DATE DUE

APR 2 7 1984			
JUN 1 9 1984			

DATE DUE

Successful Artist Management

Successful Artist Management

By Xavier M. Frascogna, Jr. and H. Lee Hetherington

A BILLBOARD BOOK
An imprint of
Watson-Guptill Publications/New York

To Fran, Bernadean, and Frank

Copyright © 1978 by Xavier M. Frascogna, Jr. and H. Lee Hetherington

First published 1978 in New York by Billboard Books
an imprint of Watson-Guptill Publications,
a division of Billboard Publications, Inc.
1515 Broadway, New York, New York 10036

Library of Congress Cataloging in Publication Data
Frascogna, Xavier M.   1946–
   Successful artist management.
   (A Billboard book)
   Includes index.
    1. Performing arts—Vocational guidance.
I. Hetherington, H. Lee, 1948–   joint author.
II. Title.
PN1580.F7   658'.91'7902   78-16775
ISBN 0-8230-5000-9

Manufactured in the U.S.A.

First printing, 1978

2   3   4   5   6   7   8   9/86   85   84   83   82   81

Acknowledgments

Thanks to Paul Adler, Buddy Allen, Steve Allen, Robert Altshuler, Billy Arnell, Larry Baunach, Sid Bernstein, Marty Blackman, Nat Burgess, Buzz Cason, Mario Conti, Ezra Cook, Mike Daniel, Stewart Fine, Jim Foglesong, Greg Frascogna, Steve Gatlin, Gina Gaylord, Juanita Elefante Gordon, Frank Jones, C. W. Kendall, Barry Knittel, Al Kugler, Judy Libow, Steve Loeb, David Ludwick, Kathryn Lumpkin, David Maddox, Bill Martin, Brad McCuen, Ralph Peer, II, Diane Petty, Frances Preston, Bob Reno, Ed Shea, Roy Smith, Jimmy Walker, Larry Welch, Gerry Wood, and Rolland Yancey.

Special thanks to Toula Zouboukos for her unlimited patience and understanding.

Contents

Introduction

To say that good artists need good managers is as sublime a statement as saying that the Titanic needed a port in a hurry.

During my years with the American Society of Composers, Authors and Publishers, when signing up songwriters and publishers, I was amazed at the numbers of both who would sign contracts with other organizations—without considering ultimate ramifications—because they received a few dollars more in advance money than what we offered, even though we were offering a one-year contract, and they were offering a three-year contract.

Likewise, I'm sure that our counterparts at BMI and SESAC also scratched their heads in disbelief when writers who they'd nurtured from the early high-risk years defected to ASCAP for a few advanced dollars more.

To many creative types—those folks who like to decry commerciality and the trappings of materialism—the manager represents either an unneccessary, dollar-gulping extravagance or a necessary dollar-gulping extravagance. Neither is completely true, though the latter category comes closer to reality.

One of my friends in this creative cosmos even went so far as to write a song stating, "I'm not making my music for money. I'm making my music for me."

But the same artist became somewhat disjointed when I told him essentially the same thing: Having advanced him several thousand dollars beyond what he had recouped, I, in effect, told him that, for the present, he wasn't making his music for money, but was making it for himself.

He grew furious. He turned red. He called me the Devil. He stalked out of my office.

So much for my relations with artists.

Let's try managers.

Somewhere, deep in the heart of Texas, a well-known manager invited me up on stage to view the proceedings at an open-air concert. I left the stage voluntarily after he strong-armed a female friend of mine while she was trying to do her best job as head of publicity for CBS Records/ Nashville.

Simply stated, I don't like bad artists or bad managers.

But, conversely, I like good artists and good managers. They make the best teams. Whether it's John Denver with Jerry Wientraub, or Jimmy Buffett with Irv Azoff (and previously, Don Light), or Jerry Jeff Walker with Mike Brovsky, an artist/manager combo that's working is one of the most beautiful, and profitable, relationships in show business.

Each feeds off the other's virtues, wallows in the other's weaknesses, and longs for the other's vices. Creative and business intellects seldom merge in the same brain. When they do, it's sometimes more dangerous than advantageous.

"I handle all my business affairs myself," boasts one artist, not knowing that the time and effort he spends in dealing with business matters, if concentrated on his proven creative output, would return dividends ten times that amount.

I treat that artist with the same degree of disrespect that I show any manager who asserts, "I'm learning to play the guitar so I can relate to my clients."

The complexities of both the music side and the business side of the music business are staggering. While some artist shifts some of his energies to tangle with contracts, guarantees, or advances, some upstart Elvis with mucho talent and a good manager will steal his thunder, top billing, and ticket to the heart of America in a minute.

While some manager learns G, D, and E perfunctorily on the guitar, some ace talent-broker will have his clients in a second.

Let's let creators create and managers manage.

Which brings us to this book.

Though "Frascogna and Hetherington" sounds like a Si-cilian/Southern combo, I'm here to say that I've known them both—and they're a young, intelligent, knowledge-able, and honest team that knows the intricacies of both music and management. That's a rare coupling.

This book holds interest for those artists within and with-out the music industry. It's flexible enough to give a how-to course in self-management for those foolish enough to try it, perceptive enough to urge career re-evaluation and cri-tique, pragmatic enough to assume that money and fame don't cure all ills, and blunt enough to recognize that there are such pitfalls as drugs, alcohol, and complacency that can torpedo the most well-endowed talents.

It also addresses itself to the unique problems wrought by "the elite few who have reached the level of superstar-dom" (few) and the "new artists and managers who believe they will achieve this height" (all).

The artist/manager relationship can be the most frustrat-ing, or the most endearing, valuable relationship for both. This book will give you guidance in how to make it the latter.

Long live the latter.

Gerry Wood
Southern Editor
Billboard

Part I
Establishing
the Artist-Manager
Relationship

1.
Artist Management: What Is It?

Artist Management—a familiar term to anyone associated with the entertainment industry, but what exactly does it mean? Usually we think of a manager as the artist's personal representative. While this is generally true, it still doesn't tell us what he does or how he does it. That is the purpose of this book.

The Role of the Manager

Actually, artist management consists of anything that will help enhance or further an artist's career. This can range from comprehensive career planning or complex contract negotiation to suggesting a lyric change in a song or commenting on a new recording. The personal manager is the alter ego of the artist, he's the part of the artist the audience never sees. He's a planner, adviser, organizer, strategist, overseer, manipulater, detail man, father figure, traveling companion, and friend. His involvement in an artist's career is total in scope and crucial to its success.

In some instances, a manager may have specifically defined duties such as is the case of most business managers. This type of manager will usually not be involved in creative decisions or day-to-day details. Rather, it's his job to take care of the books, make sure the bills are paid, and be responsible for making other business-related decisions.

The role a manager plays in an artist's career is directly dependent on the needs of the artist, the capabilities of the manager, and their personal relationship. It's the type of relationship that must be molded to conform to the express wishes of the parties. No two artist-manager relationships are ever quite the same.

A question posed by many artists, especially the inexperienced one interested in avoiding payment of a management commission is, "Why do I need a manager?" The answer may often be, "Maybe you don't." However, every artist needs some degree of management, even if it's provided by the artist himself. Artists seeking successful long-term careers in show business need management for the same reasons an automobile manufacturer or bank needs one. As with these types of pursuits, entertainment is a business; a very complex and demanding one at that. Just as it takes more than raw materials for a manufacturer to be successful or cash deposits for a bank to prosper, it takes more than just talent to build and maintain a career in the entertainment industry. There must be constant planning, execution, and follow-up. A successful career is full of decisions to be made, alternatives to be weighed, and rapidly changing circumstances to contend with. There's a seemingly unending stream of people to talk to: Producers, agents, publishers, reporters, roadies, lawyers, bankers, accountants, and fans—all competing for a few minutes of the artist's time. The life of a successful artist is filled with the pressure of endless details that won't wait until next week. Dealing with this pressure, following up the details, returning the phone calls—all are part of management. It's true that a newer, less successful artist will have fewer details to worry about, but nonetheless, they'll still be present. If the artist can effectively handle these management-related responsibilities, he should be encouraged to do so. There's no sense in paying someone else to do what the artist can do just as well for himself. However, attention to detail is only part of what artist management is all about.

Another important function of management is to work

out a comprehensive long- and short-term plan based on past experience and recognition of commercial opportunity. This aspect is followed by helping to insure that this plan is executed and that results are achieved. In short, management means making things happen. The value of a manager who can create action, take advantage of opportunities, manipulate the status quo into an advantage for his artist, cannot be measured in dollars and cents. This, too, is artist management.

By now one can begin to understand why artist management eludes definition. It's more of a process than a thing. It calls for diverse skills and abilities that must be utilized on many different levels in a variety of situations. One manager's mode of operation may be at odds with another's approach, yet both may prove to be equally effective. Despite this difficulty of definition and variance of tactical approaches to artist management, we feel that this book will give the artist and manager certain principles and concepts that may be applied to provide a foundation for success.

The Qualifications of a Manager

Now that we have a better idea of what management is, let's turn to the next obvious question, "Who can be a manager?" The answer is simple: "anybody." There are no universities offering degree-granting programs in artist management. Aside from a few states, the most notable one being California, there are no requirements or qualifications a manager must meet. On the whole, the field is wide open to anyone who wants to get involved. This is one of the big problems facing management professionals as well as artists. Little or no regulation of managers opens the profession to well-meaning incompetents as well as unscrupulous con-men who earn their livelihoods victimizing unsuspecting artists. Chapters 3 and 4 of this book discuss techniques for recognizing and avoiding both types of would-be managers.

As stated before, anyone can be a manager—including the artist himself. In the formative stages of his career, it may be advisable for the new artist to practice the concept of self-management. This will be examined in more detail in the next chapter.

Many persons earn their livelihood exclusively from the personal or business management of artists. They may manage as individuals or as part of a corporate management team. Other very successful and competent managers have dual professions as practicing attorneys, accountants, or financial consultants. Because of these special qualifications or skills, they may be able to offer an artist more versatility. By the same token, the artist should be certain that these dual-role individuals are as capable as managers as they are in their primary professions. A basic requirement is practical experience in entertainment management. Booking agents, record producers, and music publishers may also double as artist managers, though here the artist should guard against possible conflict-of-interest problems. These problems will be discussed in more depth in later chapters. In addition to these categories, friends and relatives of the artist may also serve as managers by virtue of their close personal relationship to the artist.

When selecting a manager, a new artist often may tend to choose a friend or relative, rather than seeking a professional with whom he has had no prior relationship. This is natural and understandable, but it may not be in the best interest of the artist's career. Often a friend or relative, while being well-meaning, will not possess the knowledge, experience, or contacts necessary to further the artist's career beyond a limited point. There's also the danger that, because of this close personal relationship, a friend or relative could not stand up to the artist and tell him "no" when firmness and objectivity are required. A "yes man" may be an asset to an artist's ego, but he's certainly of no value to his career development. This is not to say that a friend or relative may not prove to be the right manager for a particular artist. We're only suggesting that the artist should make a special effort to view a friend or relative objectively when assessing his strengths and weaknesses.

What a Manager Is Not

While a manager will have many varied duties and responsibilities, there are certain things that he should not be expected to do to earn his management fee, unless specifically agreed to by the parties.

A manager is not a booking or theatrical agent. It's traditionally not his responsibility to seek employment for the artist. This is the function of an agent specializing in this type of work who collects a fee that's separate and distinct from the manager's fee. It's the manager's responsibility to locate agents willing to seek employment for the artist and to accept or reject and coordinate the artist's personal appearances with those agents. This isn't to say that a manager may not be directly responsible for a booking now and then because of certain opportunities or circumstances, but the artist should remember that the manager is traditionally under no obligation to do this.

Likewise, a manager is not normally a record producer. If he does fill this dual role by virtue of special expertise and experience in this area, the artist and manager should work out provisions in the management contract for fair compensation for these additional duties.

A manager shouldn't be expected to promote, exploit, and administer copyrighted musical compositions written by the artist. This is the function of a music publisher. As in the case of dual record production and management, there are usually separate forms of compensation to cover these added responsibilities.

In certain situations, an attorney or accountant who also serves as a manager will command a higher percentage or fee because of his added dimension of specialty and additional services. This isn't to say that an artist's manager must also act as his attorney or accountant merely because he possesses this special expertise. This is a matter that must be determined by the parties to the management contract.

In addition to these major overlapping areas, the manager should be distinguished from a public relations man, graphics specialist, choreographer, recording engineer, studio musician, side man, road manager, or collaborating songwriter.

It's also important that the artist understand that a manager is not a banker. He shouldn't be expected to make loans or gifts to an artist or to pay the artist's expenses out of his own pocket. Expenses of the artist, as well as any direct out-of-pocket expenditures that may be paid by the manager in behalf or in connection with the artist, should ultimately be borne by the artist.

Summary
It's the manager's responsibility to work with all the various persons enumerated above in the coordination of their respective functions as they relate to the artist. The manager should be viewed as the artist's personal representative, authorized to act in his behalf when dealing with these and others in the entertainment industry.

When the artist negotiates with prospective managers, it's important to discuss exactly what the manager is and is not expected to do. Each party to the artist-manager relationship must understand the role of the artist and manager and the expectations shared by both. A clear understanding of these points is an absolute necessity to any meaningful professional relationship.

2.
The First Step

The first step for any artist striving toward a successful career in entertainment is to evaluate and recognize his particular management needs. The obvious questions that an artist should ask are: "Do I need management? If so, what type and to what degree? What are my alternatives?" The answers to these questions can only be supplied by the artist himself after careful examination of his goals and circumstances. The purpose of this chapter is to help the artist find those answers.

"Do I Need Management?"
The answer to this question is dependent on the answer to another question: "Do I seriously want to pursue a career in entertainment." If the answer to this particular question is "yes," then, without a doubt, the artist needs some form of management. If the answer is "no," there's an honest acknowledgement of the fact that singing, dancing, acting, or playing a musical instrument is a hobby; something done primarily for personal satisfaction and enjoyment. If this is the case, you need not read beyond this page.

Whether or not an individual or group is serious about a career in show business is a difficult question to answer. Almost everyone who has a talent for singing wonders at times what it would be like to live the glamorous life of a re-cording artist. Anyone with ability to play a musical instru-ment has probably given some thought to playing profes-sionally at recording sessions or on the concert stage. The dream of wealth and fame touches us all. On the other hand, few people take into account the tremendous per-sonal sacrifice, the long, thankless hours of hard work, and the years of rejection and frustration that go into making it to the top and staying there. Even assuming that an artist is willing to give the effort and make the necessary sacrifices, there's no guarantee that any artist will be successful. Thousands of talented people have struggled for a lifetime, only to remain in the shadow of obscurity. This is the cold, hard reality of the unpredictable and often cruel world of show business.

Even for the few who do make it to the top, their own hard-won success has the potential to destroy them as art-ists and as persons. This is the side of the entertainment in-dustry that is seldom seen by those outside the business, but it's reality nonetheless. Anyone considering entertain-ment as a profession should consider this aspect of the in-dustry along with the potential for rewards that are much more visible to the general public.

The degree of commitment to a show business career is a factor that can be controlled only by the artist. A number of artists are willing and able to throw themselves totally in-to a full-time career. But many more artists are unable to financially support themselves from their entertainment-oriented income, especially at the outset. As a result, they often hold part-time jobs or pursue dual careers while work-ing toward their career development goals. The manage-ment principles contained in this book are equally ap-plicable to both types of artists and may be applied regard-less of financial resources. What's important is not a per-son's financial status, but rather his talent and desire to make it. Without this, management principles and concepts are worthless.

Once an artist has decided to seriously pursue entertain-ment as a profession, he need only make a determination of the type and degree of management suitable to his particular circumstances. Regardless of the artist's talent or specific goals, he'll need to employ management principles to fully develop that talent and to realize those goals. For those not yet convinced as to the need of some form of management, let's consider the alternative—no management. "No management" means no planning, no organization, and no attention to the day-to-day details relating to the artist's career. The result of such non-action is an aimless drift of one's career from one haphazard encounter to the next. No artist can have a realistic chance at success by taking this approach.

What are the management alternatives available to an artist? Basically, there are three: self-management, limited management, and total management. The particular needs of the artist, coupled with his financial and creative circumstances, provide the answer to which alternative he should select.

Self-Management

Self-management simply means that the artist will function as manager of his own career rather than retain the services of a separate individual or firm. Every artist should practice self-management if he doesn't intend to seek outside help.

Self-management may often be the most suitable alternative to a new artist who is in the "break-in" phase of his career. Often, his management needs are not sufficiently demanding to require a full-time manager. This is also a very attractive alternative for the artist not financially able to pursue his entertainment career on a full-time basis.

Another obvious advantage to self-management is that it's less expensive than hiring someone else to provide the same service. It also provides the artist with more decision-making freedom that might not otherwise be present. Self-management avoids the need for interplay and communication between artist and manager. This is often a plus in certain instances because it closes the gap between planning and execution.

Probably the greatest disadvantage of self-management is that many artists simply don't have the experience and expertise needed to effectively manage their own careers. This is especially true of new artists. An artist in the "break-in" phase needs an experienced hand to organize and develop his career. An artist can avoid many costly mistakes and save a great deal of time by taking the advice of a seasoned manager.

Another problem is time. It takes a great deal of time to properly organize and map out long- and short-term career strategy, as well as to attend to day-to-day activities. When the artist is already spending much of his time in rehearsal or personal appearances, his management needs often suffer.

The third problem of self-management is a lack of meaningful contacts with industry professionals. A significant part of a manager's value is his ability to obtain exposure for the artist, which is often done through contacts with others in the industry. The new artist usually doesn't have these contacts.

Even though self-management isn't always the best approach, it's always preferable to no management. The principles contained in this book provide the self-manager with a basis for developing his own particular program. As his career develops, he may eventually abandon or modify the self-management approach by utilizing a form of limited management or securing the services of a full-time total manager.

Limited Management

A second alternative available to the artist is that of limited management. This approach involves retention of a person other than the artist to provide certain specific management services. The artist performs all other management functions not specifically delegated to the manager.

The most frequent example of limited management is the business manager. He's usually concerned only with business or financially oriented matters. The business manager, in most instances, has no input into creative decisions or day-to-day operations. His role is restricted to that of a business advisor and consultant. He's usually responsible for payment of salaries and expenses, insurance, banking relations, and other business-related matters. In short, it's his responsibility to manage the income generated by the artist. In some cases, depending on his qualifications and relationship to the artist, he'll also advise the artist on tax planning and personal investments. Since his activities are more restricted than those of a personal manager, his compensation will usually be less. Compensation is normally based on a percentage of earnings or a flat hourly, monthly, or annual fee.

There are other applications of limited management that can prove beneficial to the artist, while stopping short of a total management involvement. An example is a consultation arrangement with an established manager at a fixed hourly rate. This permits the artist to benefit from the manager's knowledge and experience through periodic consultation sessions while not having to pay a percentage of his earnings as compensation. Because of the limited nature of the relationship, the manager wouldn't be involved in the day-to-day details of the artist's career. He'd only serve as an advisor and counselor, much like an attorney rendering advice to a client.

Limited management relationships can be structured to fit the particular needs of artist and manager. This approach is often an effective bridge between the two extremes of self and total management. It should be considered by the artist as a potential solution to his individual management needs.

Total Management

The third major management category is the total management concept. This approach to artist management usually involves an individual or management firm that is totally involved in the creative and business development and maintenance of an artist's career. The total manager, often referred to as the artist's personal manager, is concerned with the total picture. His responsibilities usually include ultimate decision-making authority with regard to every aspect of the artist's professional life. The personal manager is in charge of day-to-day operations ranging from major policy decisions to seemingly trivial details.

Total management is preferable to other management forms previously discussed, provided that the artist's career requires this type of full-time attention and that the artist has the means to pay for it. Clearly, the established artist is the type of performer most in need of total management; however, any artist whose career is sufficiently complex can benefit from the total management approach.

3.
Finding a Manager/ Finding an Artist

Once an artist decides he needs some form of management that he's not capable of providing himself, he must then decide how to fill that need. The solution to these management needs will never be the same for any two artists because of differing circumstances, goals, and personalities.

Finding a Manager: The Artist's Perspective
Generally, there are two directions available to the artist in search of management. He can either take affirmative steps to seek out the best available management situation for him, or he can take a passive approach and wait to be "discovered." The first approach is by far the most realistic. This isn't to say that so-called "discoveries" haven't happened before and won't happen again, but the odds are slim indeed. In fact, there's a far greater likelihood that being "discovered" could be the worst thing that could happen to a young artist's career. The following example illustrates this point.

A good local rock group that could be based in any city or town in the United States, has been together for about a year. All the group members are either freshmen in college or seniors in high school. As musicians, they're better than average, having played in smaller bands in high school. In the past few months they've become a hot attraction at colleges and clubs in their area. For the first time since any of them started playing professionally, they're making some money.

The scene focuses on one of the top local clubs, where the group is playing to a packed house. The band is having a good set. The music is tight, their stage presence has finally come around, the audience is enthusiastic. The group has never been better. On their first break, they're surrounded by admiring fans. Suddenly, they're approached by a man who looks older and a little more "hip" than the rest of the audience. He introduces himself, telling them that he's a personal manager who just happened to be in the club. He thinks the group is one of the best he's ever heard. The manager is positive that a friend of his at a major record company would be interested in them if he heard their original material. In fact, if they'd sign a management contract with him, he could guarantee a recording contract and a concert tour as an opening act for a "major" artist. Throughout the conversation, he makes reference to all the different record companies and booking agencies he's worked for and all his contacts with entertainment industry executives. One thing leads to another and before the night is over, the group has signed a seven-year management contract that they can barely read, much less understand.

For the next couple of weeks, things are fine with the group. They're sure that in a few more months they'll be the hottest new act in the country. But this optimism begins to fade when the group finds out their manager's friend that was to sign them to a recording contract is no longer with the record company. Their prospects continue to dim when the manager tells them they're not quite ready for concerts yet and need more work in clubs. Little by little, they find out that the manager who was to make them stars actually knew less about managing their career than they did themselves. Loss of enthusiasm is replaced by total disillusionment. The manager has lost interest in the group but refuses to give them a release from their contract. All the while he eagerly collects his management commission, even though he has done nothing on behalf of his clients.

Within a year, the group that had so much potential and high hopes breaks up because of dissention and mistrust brought on by this unfortunate situation. The group members go their own ways, cynical and hurt. They're turned off to the music business and to anyone that even mentions the word "contract."

An extreme example? Not really. It happens more than most people are willing to acknowledge. While there are many honest, capable young managers who approach artists in clubs or recording studios and go on to establish long and successful relationships, there are many more would-be managers who fit the mold of the fast-talking, over-promising con-man in our example. This is indeed unfortunate for the legitimate manager because it makes his job more difficult.

The moral of the story is simple—an artist must be careful. He must never make impulse decisions on a matter as serious as the management of his career. If an artist is approached by someone claiming to be a manager who says he's interested in him and his career, the artist should look for certain tell-tale signs of a con-man. Does he want to sign the artist on the spot even though artist and manager are total strangers? Does he offer the artist instant fame and success? Is he unrealistic in his promises? Does he make success sound easy? If this is his approach, the artist should beware!

A legitimate professional will never offer to sign a total stranger. He'll want to know as much about the artist's background as the artist would want to know about his. If the prospective manager is for real, he'll want to set a meeting away from the club or studio to get to know the artist better and to discuss the artist's needs and his ideas on development of his career. He shouldn't mind giving the artist background about himself the artist can verify. A legitimate manager won't offer to make an artist an instant success, but will instead offer to work with the artist toward success. A competent professional won't ask an artist to sign a contract until the artist has had a chance to discuss the terms with the manager and consult a lawyer. These are things any artist should consider and look for in a potential manager. If the would-be manager doesn't pass these basic requirements, chances are that he's a fraud or a well-meaning incompetent.

One very effective technique available to the artist who has been approached by a fast-talking, big promiser is simply to ask the question, "How?" "How are you going to secure a recording contract for me? How are you going to get me a major concert tour? How are you going to make me a star? A professional's response would be, "I can't guarantee you any of that. From what I've seen and heard, I think you have potential and I'd like to explore with you the possibility of working together to realize that potential." This is the answer an artist should be looking for. Remember, all the professional should be trying to do when he approaches a new artist is to open the door to establishing a relationship. This makes the next step, which is the preliminary exploratory conference, possible. The con-man, on the other hand, is trying to pressure the artist into signing a contract without doing any research or advancing any realistic plan for achieving his career goals. Most of the time, this type of manager won't even know or care what the artist's goals are. All the artist represents to him is a quick commission or the chance to get rich if the artist does get lucky and makes it through his own efforts. The best advice to give any artist faced with this type of situation is simply to look before he leaps and when he does make a decision, be sure that he keeps his eyes wide open.

Taking Action. The alternate path to establishment of a sound and successful management relationship is through a well-planned program of affirmative action. We assume that, at this point, the artist has recognized that he has management needs but isn't sure what the next move should be.

Before doing anything else, the artist must first determine exactly what his needs are. Do I need total management or is my weakness in business management? An artist may not need a manager at all, but instead, only an attorney, accountant, banker, or business advisor.

While the artist is making a determination of his management needs, he should at the same time define his career goals with the questions: "Where do I want to go with my career? Do I want to place more emphasis on recording? Do I want to concentrate on personal appearances? Do I want to spend my time writing songs? Do I want to do all of these things?" The answers to these questions will further define the type of help the artist needs. This self-analysis may indicate that the artist needs a record producer, booking agent, or music publisher instead of a manager. Likewise, these career goals may indicate the artist needs a manager in addition to these other persons.

This type of analysis will also indicate what type of manager is needed. If the artist is oriented towards country music and has no recording affiliation, he'll want a manager who works in the country music field who can help him get a producer and ultimately a recording contract. If the artist is an established rock act with diminishing record sales and popularity, he'll want someone knowledgeable of the rock-music field who can help devise and execute a plan for career resurgence.

Selecting a Manager. Once management needs and career goals are determined, the next step for the artist is to identify prospective managers who would be best suited to give him the particular type of assistance required to fulfill his needs and help him realize his goals.

One of the best sources of information regarding potential managers are entertainment industry professionals such as film- and record-company executives, booking agents, music publishers, entertainment attorneys, and accountants. These people possess knowledge of and contacts with successful managers. They're in a position to recommend potential managers to the artist. In some instances, depending on the circumstances, they may even offer to make personal introductions or set up appointments between the artist and manager. For this reason, the artist should make an effort to get acquainted with those persons involved in the business aspect of entertainment. They can be valuable people to know.

Another source that may be of some help are organizations such as the Conference of Personal Managers that will give the artist information on member managers as well as instructions as to how and where they can be contacted.

If the artist doesn't have access to knowledgeable individuals involved in the entertainment industry, he may consult various directories and listings of personal managers such as Billboard's *Talent In Action.* These directories are usually published annually and contain valuable information regarding managers and management companies. In this directory, there's also a section devoted to artists. Under each artist listed, there'll usually be a notation of the artist's personal manager or management firm. An artist in search of management can tell a great deal from an analysis of a manager's clientele such as: how many artists he represents, what type of artists he represents, the field of entertainment in which he specializes, such as rock artists, comedians, actors, etc., and how effective he is based on the success of his clients.

These directories, while helpful, don't tell the full story. Many successful managers aren't listed because of personal preference, especially those who aren't seeking new artists because of commitments to their present clients. Also, attorneys or accountants who also serve as managers may, for professional reasons, not be listed. Artists should also note that a listing in such a directory isn't an endorsement or assurance of a manager's competence. These publications merely publish the names and addresses that are sent to them.

If the directory is used, it should be used as a point of departure. An artist should investigate those persons he may be interested in thoroughly, and never assume they're competent professionals merely because they have a listing. And never assume they're the only managers available just because they're listed in the directory. The information an artist can gain from a directory can be very valuable as long as it's viewed in the proper perspective. With this preliminary information in hand, the artist is now able to narrow the list of prospective managers he'll want to personally contact.

Getting the Appointment. Probably the most difficult problem confronting an artist, especially a new or relatively unknown artist, is getting that first appointment with an established manager. As with any other successful businessman, the established professional will most likely be surrounded by secretaries and assistants whose job it is to screen him from every new artist who wants to convince him he should manage his career.

Undoubtedly, the best way to break the ice is through a mutual friend, preferably another entertainment professional whose opinion the prospective manager respects. This sets the stage for the artist by putting the manager in a receptive mood before he even meets the artist. While this method of "getting in the door" is the best, it's generally not going to be available to most new artists unless, for instance, they're already under contract to a major record company, motion picture or television studio, booking agency, or publisher who has a direct interest in helping the artist obtain quality management.

If this option is unavailable, the next best approach is for the artist to go directly to the manager through letters, phone calls, or any other way that he can get to the manager. But he should be prepared for disappointment. Rarely will the switchboard put an artist through to the top man on the first try. The artist will often have to convince a subordinate that the boss should talk to him personally. The key here is persistence without becoming a pest. If every unknown artist gave up trying just because someone told him "no" or put him off, there'd be very few stars around today.

Assuming that the artist has secured the initial appointment, he should remember that the purpose of that appointment is merely to introduce himself to the manager and lay the groundwork that will lead to the preliminary exploratory conference. He should be brief and to the point, and not waste the manager's time. He should remember that he's merely trying to make a good first impression and create curiosity in himself as an artist. He should be organized, concise, and businesslike.

Above all, the artist should be prepared. Before initial contact is made with a prospective manager, he should prepare a kit that includes a cover letter stating who he is and his purpose. It's important that the artist convey to the manager how he came to select him. If the artist was referred by a friend of the manager or industry professional, he should mention that fact in the letter. At the very least, the artist should cite recommendations from within the industry. He should mention the names of the individuals making the recommendations, especially if they are well known and respected in the industry. He should not mention a name if it would be meaningless.

The cover letter should list the artist's name, address, and telephone number, as well as mention that a kit is enclosed containing pictures and information about the artist. The kit should contain at least one 8″ x 10″ (20 x 25 cm) photograph of the artist, a brief one- or two-page biography setting forth the nature of his act, his past experience and other relevant information (e.g., does the artist write his own material, has he been associated with other name acts, and so forth), and a brief statement of the artist's goals and management needs. Other items that could be included are trade press or newspaper clippings, a list of important past appearances, as well as information on future bookings, especially those the manager could attend. Another must for this kit is a tape of two or three of the artist's best songs or routines. The tape should be as professional as possible. Remember, the manager will be making his all important first impression of the artist based on what he hears and sees. An artist rarely gets a second chance to make a favorable impression.

This type of presentation, combined with the artist's ability to conduct the first phone conversation or personal interview in an organized, articulate, and businesslike manner will improve the chances of the manager becoming interested in the artist. The manager will appreciate the fact that the artist is professional in his approach to the entertainment business, has at least a basic understanding of the importance of management and organizational ability, and, above all, that he's realistic as to what a manager can and can't do for an artist.

This type of initial performance has the tendency to separate the potential long-term artist from the thrill-seekers and amateurs that a professional is not interested in and tries to avoid. Provided that the ability and talent come through on the tape, pictures, and other components of the kit, the artist making this type of presentation will probably rate a closer look by a management professional. If the artist can accomplish this, he has cleared a difficult hurdle in the establishment of a successful artist-manager relationship.

Every artist should be cautioned that the all-important first impression can cut two ways. An artist can cause himself immense harm in the initial interview by making certain fundamental mistakes. He should never be rude or arrogant, make demands for large advances, or harbor unrealistic goals. He should know when to talk and when to listen. Even if an artist may have tremendous talent and potential, it's of no interest to a professional manager unless the artist's attitude matches his talent. Talent is everywhere. It's the development of that talent that concerns a manager. The artist must be realistic, cooperative, and willing to work hard to develop his career. An experienced manager can usually tell a great deal about attitude from his first impression of the artist. If it's bad, the manager won't waste his time on a second meeting.

Hopefully, at this point, the manager will want to see the artist in person or listen to more material. It's at this stage that the artist should begin to apply the principles set forth in the next chapter on the preliminary exploratory conference.

Trying Again. However, in the event the artist is unable to establish personal contact with a particular manager, he should continue to try different approaches to make that all-important initial contact. Resourcefulness, ingenuity, and persistence must be relied upon. Nothing is going to happen unless the artist makes it happen.

If the artist is successful in making initial contact but the manager shows no interest, the artist should seek the manager's advice as to how he can strengthen his weak points so as to be of interest to the manager at some future date. An artist can obtain priceless information if he listens to what an experienced manager has to say. If the manager feels that the artist is talented but that he personally doesn't have adequate time to devote to the artist, he may possibly refer the artist to other managers or entertainment professionals.

Regardless of the outcome of the initial contact with a manager, the artist should strive to establish and maintain a good rapport with him. Often, this initial contact can be the first in a series of "breaks" that will lead to the realization of the artist's goals. It's also possible for the artist to establish contact with a manager who may not be interested today but may very well be interested in the same artist a year or two later, after the artist has had time to develop and mature.

Although it's easier to give advice than to take it, the artist shouldn't react to rejection in an immature or angry manner. Instead, the artist should look for ways to cultivate, refine, and improve his talent and his approach to management executives so that the next time, the response will be the desired one.

Finding an Artist: The Manager's Perspective

Managers, especially younger and less experienced ones, have many of the same problems of new artists. Finding a promising artist who possesses talent, a realistic view of the industry, and a willingness to take advice and work hard to further his career is not easy. It's even more difficult when a manager doesn't have the same level of experience or track record and resulting public acclaim and reputation seasoned managers may have.

Getting a Start. The question is often posed: "I want to get into management, where do I start?" Just as in any other profession, in order to be effective and successful, the manager must pay dues just like an artist. He should gain practical experience in the entertainment business before trying to manage professionally. Any experience in the business is valuable, whether it be in management, booking, recording, engineering, producing, public relations or any of a number of other capacities. It gives him a feel for the environment in which he'll be operating. It allows him to meet others in the industry with whom he'll be dealing. It will give him practical knowledge that will be put to use daily when representing clients.

Another form of dues paying is education. To be effective, the manager will be expected to understand or at least be aware of many complex business, financial, and legally based subject areas. He must be able to make important business decisions and to deal knowledgeably and effectively with attorneys, accountants, and bankers. The manager must be able to communicate with others, to express himself orally and in writing on numerous levels. For these reasons, formal education or a college degree, while not essential to success, gives him a tremendous advantage.

Attracting Clients. Aside from developing qualifications and gaining experience, the more direct question is, "how can I as an aspiring young manager, attract clients?" Probably the best way is through industry professionals such as film and recording executives, publishers, booking agents, producers, entertainment attorneys, or accountants. These people have the inside line on promising new artists. Through personal contact with these persons, a young manager can gain valuable information on these emerging artists.

Another method of attracting clients is through existing

clients or other artists with whom the manager associates. Artists frequently count other artists as their friends or acquaintances. The best calling card a relatively unknown manager can have is his own artist-client. An artist who believes in his manager and is satisfied with his level of performance will make this fact known to his artist friends. The artist grapevine is an effective business attracter.

A third method of finding new artist-clients is the direct or discovery approach. This means personally scouting talent in clubs or recording studios hoping to find artists with the type of potential talent and personality that would merit an investment of time and effort to develop their careers.

The problems inherent in this type of approach already have been discussed from the artist's point of view. Many artists will mistrust managers taking this type of approach for the reasons mentioned earlier in this chapter. The young manager should not overpromise or make bold statements that he may not later be able to back up. The initial approach should be businesslike and reserved, inviting the artist to meet at a later time at the manager's office.

The manager should be extremely cautious as to the type of artist he approaches. Many artists don't have the willpower, maturity, or ability to make it. This type of artist can become a burden on the manager. Although this situation is possible with any new artist, the likelihood is probably greater with artists discovered through the scouting method. In order to guard against this happening with any artist, the manager should conduct a very thorough preliminary exploratory conference in order to increase the prospects for success of the artist-manager relationship.

4.
The Preliminary Exploratory Conference

Probably the most influential force behind an artist is his manager. He is concerned with the day-to-day planning, control, and development of the artist's career. As previously discussed in Chapter 1, the function of a total manager covers a multitude of duties, with the constant center of attention being the artist-client.

The most important factor in establishing and maintaining a truly rewarding artist-manager relationship is mutual trust. The artist must have total confidence in the manager's motives and abilities. Conversely, the manager must be committed to the artist and his art form. A strong artist-manager relationship is in many ways analogous to a stable marriage. Research indicates that the longer couples date prior to entering into a marital relationship, the greater the probability for a lasting marriage. We believe this theory is applicable to a successful artist-manager relationship. A long "courtship" offers both artist and manager the opportunity to evaluate the other, hopefully resulting in mutual friendship and admiration. Without the existence of trust in the artist-manager relationship, problems will undoubtedly appear at some point in the artist's career. However, a long courtship is not always realistically possible in each situation because of the fast pace and constantly changing environment of the entertainment industry. Nonetheless, a condensed analysis of the artist and manager leading to an informed decision on the advisability of entering into an artist-manager relationship can be achieved by the use of the preliminary exploratory conference.

The purpose of the preliminary exploratory conference is to afford both artist and manager the opportunity to accumulate the various bits of information necessary to make an intelligent decision regarding entry into an artist-manager relationship. If the parties decide a management arrangement would be beneficial, the information exchanged at the preliminary exploratory conference will greatly help in determining the type of management relationship actually needed. Furthermore, this information will aid the attorneys in the preparation of the final management agreement between artist and manager.

While ideally, during this conference, time should not be a factor, in reality, time limitations will almost always exist. Nonetheless, the artist and manager must allow enough time to complete the preliminary exploratory conference phase in order to establish a solid foundation for their new relationship. Otherwise it could well be short lived, regardless of the dictates of time pressures.

It should be noted that during the preliminary exploratory conference, the parties should not negotiate the management contract. Instead, the purpose should be to gather data helpful to both artist and manager in evaluating the question of whether or not to enter into a formal management agreement.

Preliminary Exploratory Conference— The Artist's View

Assuming sufficient interest has been shown in a particular artist by a manager, the artist should request a conference to discuss business and managerial points of concern to each. Prior to this conference, the artist should have formulated the answer to three key questions.

The first question the artist should answer is, "How did I choose this particular prospective manager? Was it by recommendation of another artist or manager or by some other rational means?" To insure that the artist is intelligently pursuing a program of affirmative action in the selection of his manager, this question must be answered. Too often a manager is retained because it "just happens," or, because a person has been a good friend over the years; or is a "yes" man to the artist. While the professional manager may not be a close relative or friend at the moment, nor a "yes" man to the artist's every whim or desire, he may be the best qualified and most competent person to manage his career. By asking himself this question, the artist can reinforce his awareness of why he is dealing with a particular manager. Being a close friend or relative of an artist, should not necessarily exclude a person from being considered as a potential manager. This person should receive the same objective scrutiny as any other potential manager. Because of the profound effect that a manager has on an artist's career, it's absolutely essential that the artist investigate the potential manager as thoroughly as possible.

Secondly, as stated earlier, the artist should know what he wants from his career. He must have a goal. Be it the desire of being the most popular country recording artist in the United States or the hottest attraction in Las Vegas, the artist can be specific in his request for managerial help only if he first has formulated his goals. Although the artist may generally know where he wants to go with his career, how to get there may be a puzzle. Quite often an artist possesses the talent to achieve a desired goal, but lacks the understanding necessary to coordinate the many factors affecting the direction of his career. This is where the management professional earns his percentage. However, before a potential manager can discuss a management relationship intelligently, he must have at least a general idea of the artist's goals.

Once the goal has been established by the artist, and the manager has acknowledged that it's a realistic goal based on the artist's talent, a timetable should be constructed. The manager should establish preliminary intermediate goals or sub-goals, and estimate the length of time required to accomplish each. Once sub-goals are established, the artist can deal with each step of his career separately. Instead of wasting his time and creative energies trying to understand the interaction of the entire entertainment industry, he can devote full attention to the attainment of his sub-goals. By complete attention to the fulfillment of the sub-goals, coupled with strict adherence to the established timetable, the manager can plot and predict the artist's estimated time of arrival at his major goal destination.

. Beware of a manager who has no answer to the "how" question. A lack of ideas regarding the construction of an artist's career plan could indicate a lack of interest in the artist, or a deficiency in expertise necessary to provide the artist with the type of help and assistance that he needs.

The third preliminary question the artist should address himself to is a general idea of what he wants a manager to do for him. This will enable the artist to compare the services offered by the manager to the artist's preconceived needs. While deviation from these management needs does not necessarily indicate the manager can't do the job, it does give the artist some conception of his own needs for purpose of discussion during the initial conference. The artist may discover that what he wants and needs is not management. It may be an entertainment attorney, banker, or producer. An awareness of what the artist is looking for in a manager will greatly help the manager to determine if he can give the artist the type of assistance his career requires.

During the actual conference phase, the artist should discuss his goals and needs in detail. He also should invite the manager to assess them to see if they're realistic.

As another key topic during the preliminary exploratory conference, the artist should inquire as to the manager's credentials and overall contacts in the music industry. While a prospective manager may be knowledgeable and experienced in the record production or booking facet of the industry, this doesn't necessarily give him credentials as an effective manager. Unless the prospective manager's reputation is well known by virtue of managing established show business clients, the artist should inquire directly, but tactfully, into the manager's capabilities and past experience.

Another often overlooked qualification in a manager is his level of formal education. Although it isn't essential that a manager have a college degree in order to qualify for artist management, it would certainly be a valuable credential. This is true not only in the entertainment industry, but in any business. Moreover, if the manager's degree is in business or psychology, the credential is worth even more to the artist. In addition, if the manager holds graduate or professional degrees, the credential value is obviously even higher.

Another critical factor in determining a prospective manager's credentials is his reputation. This can be determined, first, by asking what the reputation of the manager is in the industry. Is he respected for his ability and integrity? And second, by finding out who his clients are. Obviously, if a manager currently has one or more highly successful clients, his reputation is enhanced.

Another method of measuring a manager's value is by observing his involvement in various organizations. Is he a member of the Conference of Personal Managers or other important trade organizations or associations? Does he attend or participate as a panelist at music industry conventions, forums, and seminars? In short, what is his industry involvement and exposure?

An obvious question of importance to the artist is, "What does the manager want for his services?" Depending on the bargaining position of both parties, several arrangements are available. The percentage arrangement, whereby the manager is paid a percentage of the gross earnings of the artist, is the most common. The percentage will vary from 10% to 25% of gross earnings, with some managers taking an even higher percentage. The artist must determine what he can presently afford and what he's willing to pay the manager. Another approach is to set the manager's percentage at an escalating rate, depending on the amount of total gross income. As gross income goes up, so does the percentage. Alternatively, depending on the status and negotiating position of the parties, a management percentage could decrease as gross earnings increase. Each particular arrangement is as unique as the parties themselves.

Sometimes a young artist may be in a very weak financial position, incapable of paying any management percentage, but in desperate need of the services of a manager. A possible solution here is the retainer method of compensation. Instead of paying the manager a percentage of all monies received, a flat or fixed sum is paid to the manager, either weekly or monthly. Although the retainer may be much less than a set percentage of gross earnings, it might possibly be adequate compensation to bring the artist and manager together during the artist's early struggling years. Hopefully, with the help of a competent and effective manager, the artist's earnings will increase to a sufficient level to allow conversion to a percentage of gross earnings arrangement.

In some cases, a manager might offer his services for no compensation at all until the artist earnings reach a certain level, and thereafter take a higher percentage than normal to make up for this time. But this has a disadvantage. While it may appear that the artist is getting a "great deal," the actual net cost to him could be substantially higher. Another pitfall in the non-payment situation between artist and manager is a lack of commitment of both parties. If perhaps an artist's business is not being attended to properly, he's in a weak position to voice complaints. However, upon the payment of a fee or percentage which has been agreed upon and accepted by the manager, that artist has standing to advance any complaint whatsoever pertaining to the handling of his career and business affairs.

Another important aspect that requires evaluation during the preliminary exploratory conference is the personality of the manager. The personalities of the artist and manager must be compatible. Can the artist relate to the manager? Can the manager communicate with the artist? Without the ability of each to exchange ideas, it will be almost impossible to achieve an atmosphere of trust. The artist and manager must be able to communicate, and successful communication will be greatly affected by the personalities of the parties involved. Therefore, in a situation where the artist hasn't had a great deal of contact with the prospective manager, the preliminary exploratory conference gives him the opportunity to discuss the types of topics that require candid communication (i.e., compensation of the manager). If a feeling of free-flowing communication with the manager isn't felt by the artist during this conference, an extremely cautious approach should be taken beyond the conference stage. However, a lengthy preliminary exploratory conference could quite possibly open up the channels of communication between the artist and manager as their personalities adjust to one another.

A key factor in the success of the artist's career is the manager's view of the artist. Unless the artist and manager have a basic understanding as to what they want the artist to be, conflicts could develop early in their relationship. Therefore, it's important to ask how the prospective manager views the artist. Since the answer to this question will determine the structure and content of the manager's overall career plan, the parties should devote the time necessary to adequately define the artist's image.

The artist should be aware of his (or his group's) strong points and weaknesses. If the manager has seen the artist perform or is familiar with his career in general, he'll probably have some opinions along these lines. A management professional who is not familiar with the artist will discover the strengths and weaknesses of an artist either through the preliminary exploratory conference, or from others in the entertainment industry. Failure to accumulate this information would make the formulation of a comprehensive career plan virtually impossible.

Another question that should be raised during the preliminary exploratory conference pertains to a manager's potential conflict of interest. Simply stated, he should be asked, "Do you have any conflict of interest that might have a detrimental effect on the artist's career?'' For example, a manager may also be a producer, publisher, or booking agent. Although various state statutes, musicians' union, and management association guidelines prohibit the overlapping of a manager's involvement in other areas such as booking, such overlap does take place. While the artist should be cautious in defining such areas, they shouldn't necessarily be construed as negative in themselves. Many times, the fact that a manager owns or has an interest in a recording studio, booking agency, or production company can be beneficial to his artist-client. The artist should simply define the overlapping of functions to insure both parties that the questions of conflict of interests can't be raised later in the artist's career. Once the parties are fully aware of any possible conflict and have constructed the terms of the artist-manager agreement accordingly, a potential conflict of interest issue will be minimized.

Another question to ask is, ''How inquisitive is the potential manager during the preliminary exploratory conference?'' An experienced manager will want to know all that he can about an artist. He'll ask a multitude of questions, seeking to accumulate personal and business facts in order to construct the preliminary career plan. Beware of the manager who doesn't seek information about the artist. Without it, a plan cannot be drawn, and without a plan, there's no management. An astute and competent manager will want to know about the artist's career history and financial condition, both professionally and personally. Does the artist have an accountant? Does he have life insurance, equipment-vehicle insurance, and so forth?

Once the artist has been through the preliminary exploratory conference stage, he'll have a first impression to evaluate. Needless to say, a positive or negative one will result. Pending either, he should take a couple of weeks, if possible, to think about the preliminary exploratory conference meetings and the exchange of ideas and information between him and the potential manager. He should review the manager's ideas, proposals, and suggestions; the manager's view of the artist, and his credentials. Also, the artist should review his goals and preconceived ideas about what a manager should do in light of his ideas on the subject. Then, he must make a decision.

Preliminary Exploratory Conference—
The Manager's Viewpoint

The formulation of a good artist-manager relationship is a two-way street. Both parties must be happy. Therefore, the investigatory process during the preliminary exploratory conference is just as important for the manager as it is for the artist. He, too, can gain a valuable insight into the attitudes and ambitions of the artist so he'll be in a better position to make a decision to reject or accept the responsibility of developing the artist's career. Basically, the manager's questions during the preliminary exploratory conference should center around certain key areas.

Just as in the case of the artist, the manager should ask himself, "Why did the artist come to me? Was he recommended by one of my artist-clients, or by a professional within the industry?" Quite possibly, the artist and manager may have been working together in another capacity (e.g., artist-publisher) for many years and the need for management may have arisen just recently. Whatever avenue the artist has traveled to reach the manager, he must know how the artist arrived in his office. First of all, from a negotiating standpoint, this information can be most helpful. If the artist was attracted to the manager because of his excellent reputation, obviously he'd be in a strong negotiating position. Alternatively, if the artist was approached by the manager, his negotiating position would be somewhat diminished. In addition, if the artist and manager have had the opportunity to work together in the past in another relationship, chances are that they're already quite familiar with many of the areas to be covered in the preliminary exploratory conference. This, of course, is good. However, the conference is still necessary in order to review the many aspects found only in a management relationship.

The manager should next evaluate his managerial talent and style in relation to the prospective artist-client. For example, if the manager's strengths are in the country music market, he should be extremely cautious of signing a hard rock attraction. Each aspect of the entertainment industry is complex. For a manger to be a true professional in his area, he must know the components and structure of the particular segment of the industry in which he operates as well as the people who comprise that segment. Unless the manager has the requisite knowledge and contacts of the segment required by the artist, he cannot adequately represent that client.

Not only does the business necessitate specialization, but so does the communication process. Communication between a hard rock manager and a country artist may in some cases prove to be difficult. Even given a unique relationship between artist and manager, potentially, the characteristics of a hard rock manager could be detrimental to the country-oriented artist-client when dealing with record label representatives, disc jockeys, and booking agents totally involved in the country field. A manager capable of "wearing several hats" is certainly not impossible to find; however such a versatile individual is not common. In short, the manager must be aware of his own capabilities and limitations when considering signing a new client.

The manager's perception of the artist and his art form must be analyzed. The manager must believe in the artistic work of his client. Artist and manager must be on the same artistic wavelength. Each must know the career direction of the artist and totally accept and be committed to that direction. For example, if a manager views his client as the successor to Alice Cooper, while the artist envisions himself as another John Davidson, potentially, this artist-manager relationship has serious problems. Therefore, the artist's image and artistic direction should be specifically analyzed and discussed during the preliminary exploratory conference.

Management compensation is obviously another important consideration for discussion. As noted in the artist's view of the preliminary exploratory conference, management compensation can take many forms. The primary point here is for the manager to know his bargaining position. In addition, if he's inclined to sign the artist, the goals and time requirements for accomplishing these objectives must be analyzed. Especially if the manager has several other clients, the time factor can be most important. Also, the financial arrangement must be equitable in terms of time input versus compensation. Ideally, from a business standpoint, a manager should view his clients like an investment portfolio, some being current revenue producers, others on the brink of financial maturity, while some going through a growth and building stage with little current return. A mixed portfolio of clients can be a strong determining factor as to the flexibility of the manager in setting his amount and mode of compensation.

In order for the manager to construct a career plan for the artist, a wide range of business-oriented questions have to be answered before a viable career plan can be formulated. The fundamental questions that the manager should ask during the preliminary exploratory conference are:

What legal entity is the artist doing business as: sole proprietor, partnership or corporation, or joint venture? Ownership entity must be established.

Are there any existing management, booking, recording, or publishing agreements in effect? If so, what are the terms of these agreements and what is the status of the artist with regard to the parties to those contracts? If there were previous agreements that are allegedly inoperative, are there proper releases evidencing such?

What are the artist's professional assets?

Is the artist a member of the proper union organization? If he is a member, but not in good standing, why?

What is the artist's personal and business debt structure?

Is the artist's name trademarked?

What are the artist's past earnings over the past five years broken down as to amount and source?

Does the artist keep proper financial records?

Does the artist have good banking relations?

Has the artist filed proper federal and state income tax returns for the last five years?

Does the artist have proper insurance coverage?

What is the artist's reputation and present image?

Does the artist write his own material? If so, is he a member of a performing rights society? Does he have a publisher?

Does the artist have any affiliate companies (e.g., publishing, production)?

What is the artist's past recording experience?

What has been the artist's market exposure, both live and recorded?

What current industry trends might influence the artist's career?

These questions are fundamental. While they don't indicate the entire spectrum of inquiry a manager could delve into relative to business planning, they're the basics. As each one of these questions is raised, additional questions will undoubtedly result. However, the expertise of various professionals, such as attorneys and accountants, will probably be needed to adequately solve the resulting problems, depending on the training and background of the manager. The manager should know his limitations and not hesitate to seek professional counsel regarding these essential matters.

Finally, but probably most important, is the personal aspect of the potential management relationship. The manager must determine what kind of personal relationship he'll have with the artist. He must ask himself, "Are we compatible? Is the artist willing to work toward his goals or does he expect me to do everything? Is the artist realistic? Does he have the ability and discipline to face the hard times as well as the good? Is he dependable? What is his reputation in the industry?" The answers to all the other questions may be good, but unless the same can be said of these questions, the manager should seriously consider if this is the kind of artist with which he wants to become involved. The pitfalls to this type of situation are obvious and should be guarded against.

The end result of the preliminary exploratory conference is a basis for the formulation of the career plan, one that's creatively self-fulfilling to the artist and financially rewarding to manager and artist.

Evaluating the Preliminary Exploratory Conference

The artist and manager should be in a much better position to evaluate each other's professional talents after the preliminary exploratory conference. At this stage, the manager should have enough data to begin to design a career plan for the artist should a management relationship result, while the artist should have a better understanding of his management needs.

No matter how long the preliminary exploratory conference takes, whether it be several days or several weeks, it should be complete. However, once this stage has ended, both manager and artist should make a decision. Procrastination doesn't enhance a good artist-manager relationship. If both agree on the direction of the artist's career and its goals and, most important, on each other, they should be eager to begin. Delay can easily be construed as a negative factor. Indecision means no decision. In short, they must make a decision. If it's yes, then they'll go to work. If it's no, then the artist will continue to look for another manager.

5.
The Management Contract

As pointed out in the preceding chapter, the preliminary exploratory conference is the device artists and prospective managers should use to determine whether or not to enter into a management relationship. If the answer to this all important question is "yes," the next step for the parties is to define and formally structure the details of their business and legal relationship. The final product of this process is the management contract.

It's often difficult for artist and manager to address themselves to delicate areas relative to financial and legal matters affecting their newly created relationship. This is especially true where there's a high level of mutual respect and admiration between them and where each has a keen desire to get to work on the artist's career development. Regardless of this reluctance, however, it's absolutely essential to the ultimate success of any artist-management relationship that a formal management contract be negotiated and executed before anything else is done.

The first step in negotiation of the management agreement lies with the parties themselves. They should meet to discuss and exchange viewpoints on how each envisions their relationship. This should include the respective role that each will play and a treatment of the specific subject areas relating to financial, business, and legal aspects of the management relationship. Such a discussion will resolve many basic areas of the relationship, while at the same time will undoubtedly pose many unanswered questions and expose new areas for discussion. We've listed below several broad subject areas the parties should concentrate on during their initial discussion. They include: the manager's duties, the artist's role, length of the management agreement, manager's compensation, expenses, accounting procedures, and prior contracts that may still be in force.

Once the parties have reached a general understanding of what they want their relationship to be, the next step is for each to seek separate legal counsel. When choosing an attorney, each party should make sure he has experience in the entertainment industry in general with special expertise in drafting management contracts. Often, artists and managers alike make the mistake of not retaining a specialist. A lawyer with no background in the field will most likely overlook or not understand many vital points of the management relationship and resulting contract.

The artist or manager shouldn't be concerned if every point is not worked out before counsel is retained or that there may be unanswered questions or differences of opinion as to specific provisions of the agreement. Such a situation will allow each party's attorney to understand and appreciate the position of his client, make a clearer determination of his needs, and allow him to advise and help negotiate the specific aspects of the management agreement.

After artist and manager have reached a basic agreement on the major points, they should turn negotiations over to the attorneys. The biggest mistake one can make is attempting to completely negotiate and draft a management agreement without assistance of counsel. There are several reasons for this.

The most important one is that an experienced entertainment lawyer will make sure all necessary points of the contract have been discussed and included in the final document. He'll be able to counsel and advise his client on the merits of all relevant subject areas, whether previously discussed or not yet considered. Second, the lawyer is able to act as his negotiator, sparing artist and manager from direct confrontation over delicate matters. This allows the artist and manager to preserve their close personal and aesthetic relationship while insuring that essential points dealing with such subjects as compensation, expenses, and so forth, are resolved in terms satisfactory to all involved. Finally, the entertainment attorney has the ability to draft the final agreement in clear, concise language that will help avoid ambiguities that could lead to disagreements while insuring that the parties have a legally enforceable document.

We can't stress enough, that one should never adopt a "do it yourself" approach when it comes to legal matters. It will be tempting, especially when an artist or manager is trying to save money and one of them has access to a form management agreement. However, every artist-management relationship has its own unique aspects or special twists that a form may not be capable of fully expressing. It's worth a little extra money at the outset of the relationship to insure that the management contract accurately reflects the true intent and complete agreement of the parties.

The uniqueness of each management relationship makes it difficult to draw generalizations regarding specific legal provisions. However, there are certain subject areas common to all management agreements. Our purpose is to outline and discuss these topics in order to give the artist and manager a better understanding of the scope of the management agreement and to serve as a point of reference as to subjects that should be dealt with in the preliminary negotiation phase. Moreover, a better understanding of the terms, provisions, and intent of the management agreement by the parties will assist the attorneys in drafting an instrument capable of accomplishing their mutual objectives.

Most management agreements can be divided into ten

major subject areas: appointment of authority, management compensation, reimbursement of expenses, exclusivity, terms, disputes, artist warranties, accounting and trusts, general legal clauses, and definitions.

Appointment of Authority

Generally speaking, there are four basic areas to look for in the management agreement regarding this topic: appointment, manager's duties, power of attorney, and employment agency disclaimer.

Appointment. The appointment provision usually does just what it states, appoints the manager to do certain acts. For the protection of both parties, the appointment language should be clear and specific. This provision can be used to specify the type of management relationship the parties desire; i.e., personal management, business management, and so forth. Also, the question of an exclusive or nonexclusive managerial appointment can be dealt with in the appointment clause.

Manager's Duties. The manager's duties should be specifically spelled out under the Appointment of Authority topic. The general phraseology used in many management agreements sets forth a number of managerial duties. Traditional duties of the manager are: to represent the artist as an adviser in all business negotiations and other matters relating to his entertainment career; to supervise professional engagements, and to consult with employers in the entertainment and literary fields; to cooperate with and supervise relations with any booking and literary agents whom the manager may from time to time employ with the artist's consent; to be available at reasonable times at the manager's office to confer with the artist on all matters concerning his artistic career, including but not limited to publicity and promotion; to use best efforts to arrange interviews, auditions and tryouts designed to further the artist's career; to perform, wherever and whenever possible and whenever called upon such other functions as may be consistent with any of these specific duties.

Again, it must be emphasized that these subject areas are generalizations. The duties of a manager can be made more or less specific depending on the desire of the parties. The needs of the artist or the manager's capability may totally alter the sample clauses just cited. Nevertheless, reference is made to them to help make the artist and manager aware of the importance of setting forth the specific duties and responsibilities of the manager in the agreement.

Power of Attorney. A "power of attorney" is an instrument authorizing another to act as one's agent or attorney. The power of attorney clause can be styled to fit the needs of the parties. It can be general or specific in its form. For example, the artist rarely signs personal performance contracts, endorses checks received in the course of business, deals with union organizations directly, or corresponds with royalty collection societies. These are normally the duties of a manager. However, in order to make the documents the manager signs on behalf of the artist binding, it's necessary to have a power of attorney authorization in the management agreement. As stated previously, such a clause can be general, that is, pertaining to all business matters of the artist, or specific, relating to a narrow segment of the artist's business affairs. The artist can limit the power of the manager by restricting or omitting the power of attorney clause.

Employment Agency Disclaimer. Most management agreements clearly disclaim any duty to obtain employment for the artist. While the American Federation of Musicians has lifted its regulation against agents acting as managers, other professional management organizations still oppose the dual function. The duties of a manager and agent are separate. However, during the span of an artist's career, the manager may find himself devoting a substantial amount of his time developing agency outlets for his client or, if necessary, seeking engagements directly with purchasers of entertainment where permitted by law. So while the functions of manager and agent are distinct, they can overlap if circumstances dictate. This is an important point that must be carefully studied by the manager prior to entering an agreement with an artist who needs help in obtaining engagements. The artist should clearly understand that the manager has no obligation to seek employment directly if his efforts in motivating agents to book his client fail. Of course, if the manager is also acting as an agent pursuant to another agreement, then an obligation would exist.

It should be noted at this point that certain states, the most notable of which is California, restrict and regulate this dual function. The manager should therefore consult an attorney to determine the legal consequences of acting as a manager and agent. He should also inquire into any licensing requirements of the particular state of which he is a resident or in which he may operate.

Management Compensation

Once the artist and manager have agreed on the amount of compensation to be paid for the manager's service, there are still certain questions that need answering. Several of the areas relating to managerial compensation are: establishing the percentage base, time of payment, renewals and extensions, reduction of fee in the event of the manager's death, and reimbursement of expenses.

Establishing the Percentage Base. Once the management percentage has been established, assuming this is the form of compensation utilized, the parties will need to determine the base to which the percentage will apply. Will the manager receive a fee on gross or net earnings? Will the fee be calculated only on personal performance income, or will record royalties, endorsements, and songwriter income also be included? In short, on what sources of income will the manager's percentage be based? Although managers normally charge a fee ranging from 10% to 25%, the areas of income to which this fee applies will vary. The final agreement depends on the negotiating position of the parties involved and their attitude toward the compensation provisions relative to other provisions in the agreement. To some artists, the compensation clauses won't be as important as the manager's authority and designated duties clause or some other pertinent provisions of the agreement.

Special attention should be given to the artist-manager relationship when the artist desires to utilize an affiliate firm in which the manager has an interest, such as a booking agency, record company, or music publishing company. The manager may voluntarily waive his management fee from incomes derived by the artist from his affiliate company, since he has already received indirect compensation from those firms. Alternatively, the manager may argue that the incomes earned by these companies should be treated as any other income and therefore be commissionable to the manager.

In discussing the compensation provisions of a management agreement, the artist must not only consider the percentage to be charged, but the areas of his income to be affected. Many artists are overly concerned with the percentage, while ignoring those provisions that could drastically reduce the significance of a higher percentage. In summary, an artist should always consider the percentage and the base to which it applies simultaneously.

Although common in the industry, management compensation certainly need not be limited to a percentage of income. In some instances, the artist may want to retain the manager on a fee arrangement, that is, a guaranteed amount payable at predetermined times. Such an arrangement may be more economically feasible or advantageous to the artist (or manager) than a percentage of the artist's income. Again, different circumstances will influence the final arrangement.

Time of Payment. Another important consideration is determining when the management percentage will be paid; weekly, monthly, or quarterly. When attempting to resolve this question, attention should be given to the artist's type of work. For example, an artist performing primarily on the nightclub circuit would have good weekly cash flow capable of paying management fees on a weekly basis. However, an artist playing one-nighter concert tours may elect to perform only during certain months, making it hard to maintain a weekly payment schedule. In addition, the accounting problems associated with a popular one-nighter attraction may necessitate payment of all management fees at the end of the each month, or at the end of a tour, rather than a weekly payment. Therefore, in order to alleviate any problems of nonpayment penalties in the management agreement, commissions should be structured so that the artist can pay as income is derived.

Renewals and Extensions. One provision somewhat misunderstood by many artists deals with extension and renewals. Simply stated, the provision states that if a manager negotiates a contract for the artist and revenue from that contract is received beyond the term of the artist-management agreement, the manager is still entitled to a commission of the revenue received by the artist. For example, let's assume that an artist wants to secure employment in a major hotel in Las Vegas. He contacts a manager knowledgeable of that market and requests an audition. After the audition, the manager informs the artist his act is not suitable for the Las Vegas market. However, the manager is interested in working with the artist and believes Las Vegas dates could be secured by using their joint business and creative talents. They enter into a three-year management agreement calling for the artist to pay a 15% management commission. One year later, the artist and manager have developed a show suitable for the Las Vegas market. The manager utilizes his contacts and secures a one-month engagement for his client in a major hotel. The artist does well and the Las Vegas employer books a return engagement the next year. The second engagement is so successful the employer now wants to book the artist for periods of sixteen weeks a year for three years. The manager would obviously be entitled to his commission for the engagement played during the final year of the management agreement. But what about the two additional sixteen-week engagements following the termination of the agreement? Regardless of whether or not the management agreement is terminated, the manager should be entitled to his fee on the monies received by the artist for the dates played after termination of the management agreement.

There are various ways to control, compromise, or limit the extension and renewal clauses. An attorney knowledgeable of the repercussions of these types of provisions will seek to obtain the most favorable wording possible for his client. Both manager and artist can advance strong arguments for removing or retaining these types of provisions.

Reduction of Fee in the Event of the Manager's Death. Another provision often included in the management agreement involves the amount of commission paid in the event of the manager's death. If the management agreement is with a partnership or corporate entity, this clause probably will not be included unless other circumstances dictate. Assuming, however, that the agreement is with an individual, there would be language included to protect the manager from a total loss of all income on contracts made on behalf of his client in the event of the manager's death. For example, a clause is often inserted whereby the estate of the deceased manager would receive a reduced percentage of management compensation derived from contracts negotiated by the deceased manager for the artist. This type of clause can be used in conjunction with the provisions previously discussed regarding contractual extensions and renewals that are employed to insure an equitable and fair agreement for all parties concerned.

Reimbursement of Expenses

Normally a manager is reimbursed for all direct expenses relative to a particular artist in addition to his management commission. However, this area can be structured in many ways.

The clause can be drafted accordingly, depending on the degree of control the artist wants to exercise over the manager. Money, area, time, and type limitations are just a few of the many ways to control spending by the manager. The manager may have the authority to spend up to a certain amount without the artist's approval—for example, any expenditure less than $500. Alternatively, the manager may be granted the right to spend any amount necessary for certain types of expenditures. Another approach allows the manager to spend up to a certain amount each month in artist-related expenses. This approach is normally used after a budget has been established and it becomes a matter of simply paying the regular monthly bills. Still another approach provides that the manager be reimbursed for expenses incurred only beyond a certain radius of operation. By way of illustration, let's assume artist and manager are based in New York City, but that it's necessary for the manager to spend time in Los Angeles. All expenses associated with Los Angeles trips could be recoverable, but trips within a 250-mile radius of New York, representing the majority of the manager's travel activities, are not recoverable from artist earnings.

These are just a few of the many alternatives that could be drawn into the reimbursement clause under the compensation provisions. But regardless of the approach utilized, the parties shouldn't hesitate to negotiate a contract that best characterizes their desired relationship.

Exclusivity

In most management agreements, the artist grants the manager an exclusive right of representation. However, the manager is normally not obligated to render his services exclusively to the artist. Although this type of provision is standard in the industry, it can still, in some instances, be the subject of negotiation.

The basic premise supporting this unilateral exclusivity is the unique talent of the artist. It's virtually impossible to duplicate the style and personality of any artist, especially an established artist accepted by a vast segment of a particular market. On the other hand, the manager's talents are normally business-oriented, which can be more easily duplicated or substituted. Of course, this is a generalized statement. Certainly there are managers who are just as unique, or more so, than their clients. Some managers possess business and marketing skills beyond monetary value. But generally speaking, it's the artist who has the unique characteristics. Therefore, the manager will normally insist that the artist be the one exclusively bound in the agreement.

From a practical standpoint, the manager must be free from interference from others having a stake in the artist's career if he is to keep his client moving toward his predetermined goals. One person must be the overall decision-maker and spokesman for the artist, simply to avoid confusion. While agents, publishers, producers, and public-relation firms make various decisions affecting the artist's career, they're usually made within certain boundaries established by the manager, or with his direct approval. Unless the manager is the pivot point for all decisions concerning the artist's career, a catastrophe could result. As a result of the exclusive representation clause, record executives, agents, concert promoters, merchandisers, and others know where to contact the decision maker, when he's available to conduct business on behalf of the artist. A successful artist whose days and nights are taken up with performing, traveling, writing, and recording shouldn't attempt to fill this dual role. The exclusivity clause allows his manger to perform this function.

The manager normally has other business interests; therefore, an agreement that requires the manager to devote all his time to one particular artist could be economically detrimental to the manager. Many artists are not income-producing entities when they first seek artist management. So unless the manager is deriving income from other sources, it might be impossible for him to represent a young, inexperienced artist. On the other hand, if the artist has reached superstardom, it may be economically feasible for the manager to exclusively represent just one client.

Moreover, if the artist is in semi-retirement and has the time and desire to administer certain aspects of his own affairs, a non-exclusive agreement may be beneficial. Again the circumstances of the parties at a given time will influence the content of the management agreement.

Term

The term or length of the management agreement is one of its most important points. There are numerous advantages and disadvantages to an agreement with long or short durations.

From the manager's viewpoint, a long-term agreement is beneficial in protecting the manager's investment if he's dealing with a new artist requiring a long development phase. A manager usually won't be inclined to invest substantial amounts of time to develop an artist, only to lose him once results are achieved. Conversely, a manager may not want to get involved in a protracted development phase and may seek a short-term agreement with option provisions.

The artist, on the other hand, may not want to bind himself for a long period with a new manager. However, the artist may want to enter into a long-term agreement with a well-known manager who is capable of developing the artist to his maximum potential.

The term of most management agreements ranges from one to three years with options. The option term usually consists of one to six consecutive one-year periods. An option provision means that at the conclusion of a stated time, the agreement will continue if one party, normally the manager, exercises his option. Options are often tied to certain levels of performance by the artist and/or manager. Options are recommended for the artist as a way to insure performance by the manager, especially where he may represent a full roster of other artists. Options, likewise, are advisable for the manager as a good control device.

The artist should be wary of committing his career to a manager for a term longer than three years. Time changes people and circumstances. Regardless of the strong belief an artist may have in a particular manager, he should, if possible, keep the agreement within a three-year span. If the artist is successful, a contract of short duration will allow him to re-negotiate with the manager on more favorable terms if he so desires. If the management relationship is not successful, the shorter term will allow the artist to terminate the agreement and seek alternative management representation. Use of a short-term agreement with option terms based on performance of the parties often provides artist and manager with a workable compromise that affords sufficient protection to each.

Disputes

It's good practice to include a clause in the management agreement whereby, if either party has a grievance against the other, written notification must be given and then a certain time period allowed for rectifying the matter in question before the offending party can be held in default.

However, if a controversy does arise between artist and manager that can't be settled, then an arbitration clause could be utilized. Arbitration is a procedure for resolving disputes instead of litigating the matter in a court of law. The person conducting the arbitration hearing is not necessarily a judge, but someone knowledgeable of the subject matter in controversy. The arbitration clause normally will grant the prevailing party the right to recover any and all reasonable attorney fees. Given the unique character of the entertainment industry and the crowded court dockets across the country, the arbitration clause may be beneficial to both artist and manager as a speedy, inexpensive manner of resolving disputes.

Artist Warranties

A blanket indemnification clause is usually included in the management agreement whereby the artist guarantees certain facts. For instance, let's assume that an artist, believing himself to be fully released from a previous management agreement, when in fact he really is not, enters into an agreement with a new manager. Assume further that this new management contract happens to contain a clause that warrants that the artist was free to enter into this new agreement. A short time later, a major recording contract is secured. The previous manager believes that his efforts on behalf of the artist was the reason the contract was obtained, while the new manager strongly contends that his efforts alone resulted in the contract. The result is a lawsuit between the two managers. Regardless of the outcome, under the indemnification clause of the second management agreement, the new manager would still be entitled to be reimbursed for any losses incurred by him as a result of the artist's breach of warranty. This is because the artist has guaranteed that he was free to contract with the new manager and has agreed to protect him from any loss if the manager relies on his warranty.

Accounting and Trusts

The artist should always include an audit provision in the management agreement. This gives the artist the right to examine the books of account kept by the manager. Conversely, if the artist or his representative keeps the accounting records, then obviously the manager would want the same privilege of examination. The management contract should contain a specific provision stating exactly whose obligation it shall be to keep the books of account.

As a regulatory provision to the right of examination, the audit clause should provide for a written notification and a time period for the examination (e.g., within ten days from notification during normal office hours). To avoid unnecessary or vexatious examinations, the party to be audited will often seek to limit such examinations to no more than one per year.

A trust provision places a duty on the artist or manager if either receives monies that either in whole or in part belong to the other party. The party in possession of these funds is obligated to preserve said monies until the other party is paid. Legally, this establishes a trust or fiduciary relationship which carries a greater degree of accountability between the parties involved although the management agreement would most likely be a fiduciary relationship much like attorney-client.

General Legal Clauses

All formal management agreements contain various general clauses characteristic of all contracts. For instance, a jurisdiction provision sets forth an agreement by the parties that the contract will be construed under the laws of a particular state or country. A modification clause states that once the agreement is reduced to writing and signed, then all subsequent changes must be reduced to writing and signed by both parties in order to be enforceable. An assignment and delegation clause may be found in the agreement regulating transfer of rights and duties under the contract.

Many other general legal clauses may be contained, depending on the desire of the draftsman. While these clauses may not appear to be important to a layman, they're of great importance to the attorney.

Definitions

Some management agreements contain definitions of specific words used in various paragraphs. This is done to guard against an ambiguous meaning being attached to a word or phrase frequently employed in the agreement. If the parties to the agreement are unclear as to the meaning of any word or phrase, then it should be defined. Care in drafting of the document can alleviate greater problems later on.

Summary

Different things are important to different people. Consequently, each artist and manager will be motivated by different aspects of the management agreement. Each party must know what he incorporated in the management agreement. If one party is still in doubt as to exactly what the other desires from the agreement after the preliminary exploratory conference, then he must get the advice of an attorney. The artist and manager shouldn't proceed to the next step unless both feel comfortable about the last. Remember, the management agreement can be modified to fit their particular needs. Neither party should be timid about having the management agreement tailored to his artist-management relationship. Also keep in mind that both parties must be satisfied with the end product. In a successful negotiation, everybody wins. So both parties must be prepared to give, take, and compromise so the final agreement is acceptable to both artist and manager. If it's not, then they've only ignited a time bomb that will explode in a later phase of the artist-management relationship.

Part II
Planning the
Artist's Career

6.
Taking Care of Business

Once the formal management agreement has been signed, the manager begins the actual construction of the artist's career plan. The manager's first area of concern is the artist's business condition. The artist's entire operation should be reviewed and analyzed, since the results of such an analysis will greatly influence the preparation of the career plan. The manager, in effect, must take inventory of the artist's business and creative assets. This chapter is devoted to the business portion of this evaluation. Generally, the manager's analysis should cover the following: form of doing business, employment agreements, service mark, banking, insurance, bookkeeping/tax planning, budgeting, and legal overview.

Form of Business
First, the manager should ask, "What form of business is my client currently working under?" Second, "What form of business should my client be working under?"

Basically there are three types of business entities available. They are: proprietorship, partnership, and the corporation.

Each form has its distinct characteristics. The manager should analyze the various entities in view of the artist's situation and make the appropriate selection. Often the advice of an attorney or accountant is necessary to make a determination of which form to select. As we've stated before, if the manager has any questions regarding the selection of a particular business entity, he shouldn't hesitate to seek appropriate counsel. Let's briefly review the advantages and disadvantages of the three basic entities:

Proprietorship. A proprietorship is an unincorporated business operation owned by an individual. The advantages of the proprietorship form of doing business are numerous. The primary advantage is that the owner is the boss. He makes all decisions regarding the operation of the business without having any formal meetings with others, such as a Board of Directors, which is associated with the corporate entity. There's little formality or cost associated with the formation of a proprietorship. The business is free to trade and operate anywhere without having to comply with various qualification statutes in each state that it's engaged in business. The proprietor is not subject to the liability of others, which is inherent in partnerships and with officers of a corporation. Moreover, the individual proprietor is not subject to as many regulatory and reporting requirements as are other forms of business enterprise. Finally, a proprietorship may be granted borrowing power beyond the value of the business to the extent of the owner's assets outside the proprietorship.

The primary disadvantage of the one-man business is that no one other than the owner can act on behalf of the business (except as an agent). Consequently, the business enterprise has limited decision-making capability and expertise. The owner is subject to unlimited personal liability for all the obligations of the business. Furthermore, the amount of the investment in the business is limited to the resources of the owner. Another distinct disadvantage is that the proprietorship is subject to termination upon the death or incapacity of the owner. In addition, the other entities provide certain tax advantages not found in the one-man business structure.

Partnership. A partnership is created when two or more people agree to combine their property, talent, or other resources to establish a business in which each is to be an owner sharing the profits or losses of the enterprise. While the characteristics of a partnership are similar to the proprietorship, there are major distinctions, the foremost being the general agency feature of the partnership. Every partner can act on behalf of the business, therefore rendering the enterprise liable for any partner's action within the scope of the firm's operation. Therefore, it's extremely important that each partner have the utmost confidence in the integrity and ability of his associates. Generally, the partners are liable not only collectively, but individually, for all the obligations of the business including liability resulting from wrongful acts of the other partners. The growth of a partnership can be restricted because all its members must consent before any additional members are included. However, termination takes place upon the withdrawal of any one party. If the withdrawal is in violation of the partnership agreement, it may give rise to an action against the withdrawing party, but the partnership is nevertheless terminated. Dissolution of the partnership also occurs upon the death or incapacity of one of the partners. The effect of the death or incapacity of a partner can be minimized by various provisions either embodied in the partnership agreement or by a collateral agreement between the parties. Nonetheless, if some provision has not been made, then the death or incapacity of a partner terminates the business.

Corporation. The corporate form of doing business is more complex than the proprietorship or partnership. The formation of an incorporated business creates a new entity capable of transacting business in its own name.

The major positive factor of the corporation is freedom of the shareholder (owner of the corporation) from personal liability for the obligations of the corporation. The ease in transferring ownership through exchange of stock shares is another desirable aspect of the corporate entity. An additional favorable characteristic is the ability of the corporation to exist for a set period of time without being impaired by the death or incompetency of individual shareholders. As stated previously, the ability of the corporation to do and perform almost all acts in connection with its business, which may be done by an individual, is advantageous. Finally, another major benefit is the ability of the corporation to raise large amounts of capital through investments of many shareholders.

On the negative side, the corporation is more costly to form, compared to proprietorships and partnerships. In addition, corporations are subject to more governmental regulations, such as requirements of periodic filing of reports and various statements. The fact that minority shareholders are subject to the control of the majority shareholders in the corporation can be a negative factor. Also, the credit available to a corporation is limited to its own assets, not those of the individual shareholders.

Other Business Entities. As stated at the outset, the proprietorship, partnership, and corporation are the three basic business vehicles available to the manager. It should be noted, however, there are other business entities available that are derivatives of the basic formations. Since their use is rather limited and extremely complex, these business arrangements will not be discussed. For the proper selection and formation of any of these entities, the advice of an attorney and accountant is recommended. The corporation will normally require the services of an attorney to insure that proper records are being maintained and governmental reports are being filed. The use of one of the derivatives of the major entities definitely requires counsel in their selection and formation.

Selecting the Form of Business. The manager can select any one of the various business entities available. The choice will depend on the circumstances of his client and the advice of professional counsel. For example, a young artist recently signed to a major recording contract would probably select the sole proprietorship form of business. However, as an artist's career develops, the need may arise to transform the proprietorship into a corporate entity depending on increased exposure to liability, tax consequences, and other considerations.

As another example, let's assume we're dealing with a four-man rock group. On first glance, this would seem to suggest the creation of a partnership arrangement. However, after investigation, it's revealed that one member is the financial strength of the entire group, and another member possesses all the creative, writing, and vocal talents. Given this situation, the best arrangement might not be a partnership between all four members. Instead, those members with the financial and artistic strengths may want to consider the formation of a partnership between themselves and employ the other two members. Of course, this example could be altered drastically by assuming all four members contributed equally to the group's financial strength and artistic and creative output. Furthermore, while one member may not write, he may be the lead vocalist with the unique voice capable of delivering the original compositions of the non-vocalist member. In this instance, a partnership arrangement between all four members might be the most desirable arrangement. In short, the manager must assess the artist, or the group as a whole, to determine if a partnership arrangement is the appropriate alternative for a given situation.

Before making the final decision as to which form of doing business best suits the artist, the manager should consult with the attorney and accountant. Once the manager has assessed the artist's business entity, made his recommendations, and has followed through with their implementation, the first step of the artist's business inventory is completed.

Employment Agreements
The next step is a review of the personnel requirements of the artist. For instance, if the artist is a single act, will he require a full time backup group? If the artist tours regularly,

will a road crew be required? Does the artist need a road manager? Regardless of the artist's talent and goals, he'll often require the services of other people. We shall refer to them as nonowners, or employees.

The direction of the artist and the management strategy utilized in achieving a specific goal will greatly affect the number of people the artist will have to employ. The manager must analyze the existing situation in view of how many people are presently employed, and how many are contemplated for future projects. Are all employees necessary? Does the artist have employment contracts with them?

Once the artist's needs are reviewed and the existing employee situation studied, the manager will be in a position to make personnel recommendations to his client and subsequently negotiate the employment contracts. Employee functions will vary from musicians, to music director, backup vocalists, arrangers, road manager and crew, sound engineers, stage directors, wardrobe designers, lighting technicians, vehicle drivers, pilots, bodyguards, promotion men, public relations personnel, and many others.

The manager should formalize agreements with all the support personnel employed by the artist so that both he and his client have a clear view of the financial commitment involved. In negotiating these contracts, the manager should keep in mind the artist's creative and logistic requirements as well as current and prospective financial condition.

Service Mark

An often overlooked aspect of the business inventory is the value of the artist's or group's trade name. There are many nightmarish stories about the hit group who found out they didn't have full right to use their own name. Or even more frequently, the situation exists where no partnership agreement has been executed between members of a group that subsequently breaks up. When all of the group members form new groups and utilize the trade name of the previous group, the result is protracted, expensive litigation.

The way to avoid these problems and others related to trade name use is to seek federal service mark protection by registration of the proper application with the Commissioner of Patents in Washington, D.C. The artist should simultaneously file for state service mark protection if available. The advantages are numerous. A service mark indicates the origin of the artist's services. It's a vehicle for building good-will value in the artist's business. It can be included on the artist's financial statement as an asset. It helps to protect the artist from mistake, confusion, or deceit fostered by other artists who may subsequently adopt the same or similar name. It provides insurance that the artist may exclusively perform under his professional name. In addition, it's a potentially marketable commodity. The primary disadvantage is the out-of-pocket costs associated with the filing. The manager should consult an attorney with regard to securing service mark protection at the same time he seeks advice as to the various forms of doing business.

Banking

Upon examining the condition of the artist's business, the manager needs to ascertain his client's borrowing power. The artist's relationship with lending institutions will either be good, bad, or nonexistent. Given the last two situations, the manager must convert his client into a good customer in order to establish a solid banking connection.

If the artist has never dealt with a bank before, the manager can arrange for his client to meet the proper banking officer, not only to establish a business relationship, but to insure that the artist's personal banking needs are fulfilled. On the other hand, if the artist has a poor record with a particular bank, the manager should attempt to clear up the problem, if possible, or embark on a new relationship with another lending institution. As a last resort, the manager may choose to utilize his own borrowing capacity to assist his client in starting a relationship with a bank. The shortcomings and negative consequences of the latter alternative are obvious—caution is recommended.

If the artist has maintained a good banking relationship in the past, then the manager should seek to build on the existing financial base. By meeting with the artist's banker and explaining the direction of the artist, his goals and objectives, the approach to be employed in achieving those goals, as well as the artist's budgets and forecasts, the banker will become familiar with the artist's business. Familiarity breeds confidence, and a banker's confidence in his customer is the key to borrowing capacity. The banker will be the first person to recognize professional business management. The artist can receive immediate benefit at this early stage from a manager who can explain to the banker in a businesslike fashion the objectives of his artist-client.

Once the artist's career is underway and monies are being generated, the bank can perform the normal function of moving money for necessary transactions. But beyond these normal functions are a host of services the banker can provide if he's familiar with and approves of an artist's business. Therefore, it's most important in the initial inventory that the manager establish a strong banking relationship for his artist-client.

Insurance

Various insurance coverages are an essential business tool. Any well-managed business maintains certain insurance policies for economic protection. The artist's business is no different. The manager should examine the following areas:

Vehicle Insurance. The bank will normally require insurance protection if it has financed a vehicle. From a financial standpoint, it's simply good business. But the need doesn't stop with the bank. If an artist or group has invested substantial amounts in vehicles, a total loss could result in disasterous financial consequences in attempting to replace them. Replacement problems are magnified considerably if the artist is in the middle of a tour and finds himself without vehicles or the cash to purchase new ones.

Liability insurance protection is a necessity. While the prior paragraph dealt with insuring a vehicle's property value, this deals with insuring against negligent acts of the driver of the vehicle. The many serious consequences that could result from operating an uninsured vehicle are obvious. The negative consequences are multiplied if the artist is doing business as a proprietorship or partnership due to the personal liability aspect of these business arrangements. While the members of a corporation would be protected from personal liability, the assets of the corporation are vulnerable to lawsuit arising out of the negligent operation of a vehicle owned by the corporation.

Equipment Insurance. Artists must invest substantial sums of money in their musical equipment, sound, lighting, and staging to remain competitive in today's entertainment market. Substantial equipment investments require insurance protection from fire, theft, and other potential damage or loss contingencies. The artist needs to have the assurance that in the event of equipment damage or destruction, the artist's activities can be resumed as quickly as possible without financial disaster.

Life Insurance. Life insurance coverage is another protective device that should be used by the artist. As an artist's career develops, his income usually increases. The manager and other group members (if the artist is in a partnership) become vulnerable to substantial loss of income in the event of the death of the artist or other group member. In order to insure against this contingency, life insurance can be maintained on the artist or other "key" members of the group. Such a policy would normally name the manager or the other members of the group as beneficiaries. This coverage would be in addition to life insurance in order to provide for the artist's family in the event of his death. The amount of life insurance carried can be adjusted from year to year to provide sufficient protection.

Insurance companies offer an assortment of business

coverage. The manager should ask for the opinion of an insurance expert in formulating an insurance plan to protect all the vulnerable areas of the artist's business.

Bookkeeping/Tax Planning

Is the artist maintaining a set of financial records? Has he kept books in the past? It's very important that the manager ascertain the adequacy of the artist's bookkeeping system. Not only does the manager have to concern himself with the current bookkeeping system, but it's recommended that he review the records for at least two previous years. This will help prevent any unannounced surprises from the taxing authorities. Knowledge of a client's previously inadequate bookkeeping system or of his failure to file certain tax reports doesn't mean that the manager can necessarily help alleviate these problems if the tax officials raise questions. He can, however, help avoid problems in the future.

Normally, an accountant is retained to assist the manager in installing a new bookkeeping system or reviewing the adequacy of an old one. The accountant is usually responsible for filing all state and federal income tax forms and corporate franchise and income tax returns. Unless the manager has special expertise in accounting, it's strongly recommended that an accountant be retained. The accountant will also be helpful in reviewing the artist's business as it grows to determine whether a new business form is desirable. The primary motivation for changing the legal structure of a business is usually tax implications. The accountant will be the first to recognize the tax ramifications of a particular business entity. As the artist's career progresses and his income increases, the tax consequences become more and more important in the overall career plan. The assistance of an accountant or professional tax planner becomes essential.

The manager must see that proper financial records are kept. Numerous systems are being utilized by the artist today. They range from computer systems to hand-entry records. Depending on the current income of the artist, with the assistance of an accountant, the manager can structure a system capable of fulfilling the artist's record-keeping needs.

Budgeting

A budget is a financial roadmap. Just as the road manager plots the route for an upcoming tour, the manager must map out his client's financial route.

The first step in budgeting is an income forecast. The manager must attempt to project the artist's earnings for a given year by studying the previous year's income. Once the manager has an idea of what was earned the previous year, when it was received, and what contracts are in effect for the upcoming year, he's in a position to forecast. Given the objectives of the artist, in view of the earnings forecast, the manager can determine the amount of money that will have to be generated during the year. The manager then starts manipulating the various factors (i.e., banks, agents, record companies, budget) in an attempt to provide the desired effect. For example, let's say that an artist grossed $100,000 from personal appearances and desires to increase his earnings by $25,000 for the upcoming year. The manager would have to analyze several factors. Can my client command an increased performance fee? Can the agent deliver higher priced dates? As an alternative, should the client's overhead be reduced? Should the artist shift markets? Based upon his findings, the manager will attempt to formulate an economic plan capable of fulfilling the artist's wishes.

For another example, let's assume that an artist earned $100,000 the previous year by performing in the nightclub market. For the upcoming year, the artist would like to reduce the number of nightclub performances in order to devote more time to recording. However, he wants to maintain his previous year's income. The manager has to answer several questions in designing a budget for his client. Can the artist maintain his previous year's income by working less? Should the artist cut overhead? Can the artist afford to pay the increased studio bills? Just exactly how is the manager going to help the artist accomplish his objective? Can he?

The first step for the manager is to formulate a financial plan based on a forecast and budget. The manager must be able to look into his client's economic future. From this point, he can then juggle the figures and usually structure a plan to achieve the artist's objective. But if he determines the artist's goal can't be reached, the process he underwent in reaching his conclusion will be helpful in explaining to the artist why the goal is not currently attainable.

Artists are like everyone else in that they have personal and business financial needs. It's the manager's responsibility to help fulfill those financial needs, or at least explain convincingly why the artist's desires cannot be fulfilled. It's also the manager's job to help the artist spend his money wisely in order to insure that he has something to show for his efforts once his popularity wanes.

Legal Overview

We've previously discussed the importance of attorneys during negotiation and preparation of the management contract. During the business inventory stage, any legal question regarding the artist's business status should be reviewed. The artist's manager and the attorney need to be aware of all business planning, pending litigation, existing contractual obligations, and all other pertinent legal data. The manager should consult the attorney on any matter of which he's unsure.

Once the manager has taken his financial inventory of the artist's business, he's ready to activate the business entity by preparing the career plan. This topic will be discussed in subsequent chapters.

The final result of the business inventory phase should be a well-organized, efficient business vehicle, complete with all the protective devices insurance can offer. Artist and manager should have a clear understanding of where they are financially, and exactly where they're going in the future.

7.
Attorneys, Accountants, and Business Advisors

While the manager is instrumental in structuring and administering the artist's business organization, many aspects of the artist's business will require the expertise of the professional support team. The professional support team normally consists of attorneys, accountants, and business advisors. The information and skills these professionals provide play an important part in the success of the artist's career.

A manager and artist should be aware that the entertainment industry today is a highly sophisticated and complex one, involving significant sums of money. As a result, a manager and artist can be expected to be confronted by a wide spectrum of legal and financial decisions over the span of a career.

From a legal standpoint, the artist will be involved in contractual relationships with his manager, booking agents, record company, motion picture and television producers, and advertising agencies. He'll be involved with the protection, licensing, and use of his name and likeness as well as protection, ownership, exploitation, and administration of copyrighted musical compositions and other literary and intellectual properties. A successful artist usually requires a complement of employees to help develop his career, such as musicians, road managers, drivers, roadies, wardrobe personnel, and publicity agents. He'll also be involved in the ownership or lease of sound and lighting equipment, musical instruments, vehicles, props, and wardrobe. Besides business responsibilities, the artist will also be concerned with the administration of his personal finances and investments as well as ownership of real and personal property. All of these subject areas require at least some input from an attorney.

Attorneys

As mentioned in the preceding chapter, the counsel of an attorney can be very helpful during the early stages of the artist-manager relationship. He can provide general legal counsel, contract expertise, and negotiation skills. All of these services are critical at various stages of the artist-management relationship.

Once the artist and manager have entered into a formal management agreement, the need for an attorney is still very much present. As suggested earlier, legal needs and problems will undoubtedly arise as the artist's career develops and his business operation expands. These situations will obviously necessitate the services of an attorney possessing special expertise in the field of entertainment.

The counsel of an attorney who is familiar with the historic development of his client's career can be a valuable asset to the artist and his manager. Therefore, it's sound practice for the manager to keep the attorney informed of the artist's business dealings from the very outset. A well-informed attorney will often be able to anticipate potential problems of the artist and take steps or give counsel to avoid them.

When selecting an attorney, the artist and his manager should select a person with experience in the entertainment field. They shouldn't assume that all attorneys possess the special knowledge and training to adequately handle their legal requirements. The artist and manager should realize that the trend today is toward greater legal specialization because of the increased complexity of our commercial society. Entertainment law is a specialty, the same as criminal law, litigation, or securities regulation. Unless a lawyer regularly deals with management, recording, and music publishing contracts; copyright protection and administration; and licensing of intellectual and artistic property, chances are he won't sufficiently understand the entertainment industry and its peculiar legal problems to do an adequate job for his client.

When seeking a qualified entertainment lawyer, other managers and industry professionals are good sources for recommendations as to experienced attorneys in the field. Professional directories such as *Martindale-Hubbel* may be consulted as a starting point if the artist or manager is totally unfamiliar with members of the legal profession and their qualifications. This directory is found in most law libraries, and the librarian will be glad to show how to use it. Because of the high degree of specialty of entertainment law, the majority of specialists are located in industry centers such as New York, Los Angeles, or Nashville; however, they may be found in other cities throughout the country, too. Artists and managers should be cautioned against their natural inclination to use a friend, relative, or business associate to fill their entertainment law requirements. This is fine if they're qualified. However, if they don't have an entertainment background, the manager could be doing his artist-client a great disservice by retaining such an attorney.

When contacting an attorney for the first time, it is recommended that his fee is asked about at the outset to avoid any misunderstanding. Often, the attorney will schedule an initial conference to discuss the artist's particular legal needs or problems on either a flat fee or an hourly rate basis. During this initial meeting, the artist or his manager and the attorney should discuss their financial arrangement, which will usually be based on an hourly rate or, in some cases, a percentage of the artist's income, depending on the circumstances of the artist and the preference of the parties involved.

While it's understandable that a new artist must necessarily be cost-conscious, he shouldn't neglect seeking competent, experienced legal counsel because of price. He should shop around for legal representation just as he would for any other service. It's important that he find an attorney with whom he feels comfortable, as well as one he's able to afford. Attorney's fees vary with the experience and client load of individual lawyers. Often, a younger, less experienced, though competent, entertainment attorney trying to establish himself may be just the right choice for the new artist or manager. In any event, the artist or his manager should never try to be his own lawyer just to save money, or he'll be heading for trouble.

Accountants

Just as an artist will require the services of an attorney, so will he need an accountant. One of the worst things that can happen to an artist is to experience financial success without being properly prepared for it from an accounting standpoint. There are many sad stories of artists who made fortunes, only to lose everything as a result of no record-keeping, ineffective income management, non-existent tax planning, and failure to save and make proper investments. By retaining a competent professional, this unfortunate state of events can be avoided.

We've already discussed the importance of the accountant in helping to select the artist's business entity. But, the accountant's skills in reviewing the artist's existing bookkeeping system and developing a new system if necessary are also important contributions. Of special importance to a recording artist and songwriter is the ability of the accountant to interpret and verify royalty statements. Another essential service is the preparation and filing of income tax returns with the Internal Revenue Service. This aspect of an artist's business definitely requires the skills of a trained professional. As the artist's income increases, the need for professional accounting and tax planning becomes more important. As with the attorney, the value of the accountant increases dramatically if he's familiar with the artist's business. Therefore, the manager should keep him regularly informed on the artist's financial activities.

The same general rules regarding selection and compensation of an attorney also apply to accountants, with some exceptions. While it's helpful for the accountant to have a background in the entertainment industry, especially with regard to audits and royalty accounting, it's not generally as crucial as it is with the attorneys.

Compensation of accountants varies with the expertise and experience of the accountant. A Certified Public Accountant usually commands a larger fee due to his special training and wider spectrum of knowledge and expertise. Compensation is usually based on either a flat fee or retainer basis.

Business Advisors

We'll refer to estate planners, insurance professionals, and bankers under the heading of business advisors. Their services are essential in maintaining an efficient business. The banker can play a central role in the development of a young artist's career if the manager utilizes his association with this professional properly. As mentioned earlier, the banker can provide numerous services for the artist's business and personal affairs.

The estate planner is a highly specialized professional whose function is to plan the most efficient distribution of his client's assets at death. While most artists are not concerned with this aspect of business planning at the outset of their career, it does become important later if their career proves successful. An artist must exercise caution when choosing an estate planner. There are many firms and individuals who profess to have such skills. Attorneys, Certified Public Accountants, and Chartered Life Underwriters are generally qualified to render this important service. Whoever is chosen, the artist must be certain he selects a well-qualified professional.

Summary

Selection of the members of the artist's professional support team should be given careful consideration based on professional competence and their qualifications. As with attorneys, the artist or manager may have friends, relatives, or business associates whose services they wish to employ. Again, this is fine, if they're qualified.

We cannot overemphasize the importance of the professional support team in the overall success of an artist. Remember, the entertainment industry is a highly competitive, complex business requiring the assistance of qualified professionals. The artist and his manager must select the best team they can assemble, and then listen to their advice. It will definitely be a wise investment in the future of the artist and his manager.

8.
Artist Evaluation and Image Formulation

Having previously taken inventory of the artist's business, the manager should now make a detailed creative assessment of the artist. All artists have strengths and weaknesses. It's the manager's function to identify and become familiar with these traits. This will enable him to shape the artist's image and direction in such a way so as to maximize his strong points and de-emphasize and improve on the weaknesses.

A meaningful artistic evaluation requires that the manager and artist be totally honest with each other. It suggests not only praise from the manager, but criticism also. This is no time for the artist to get his feelings hurt or let his ego stand in the way of a process that will ultimately prove beneficial to him and his career. Before the artistic evaluation begins, the manager should take steps to sufficiently prepare the artist. He should remind the artist that any criticism is meant to be constructive in nature. The manager should point out that he wouldn't be involved with the artist if he didn't believe in his talent and ability to succeed. Finally, he should stress the need for complete honesty and mutual trust. In many instances, this will be the first juncture in the relationship where there's the possibility of confrontation and friction in the artist-manager relationship.

Unless the parties understand the process and are properly prepared from an emotional standpoint, the consequences can be disastrous. By the same token, if both parties realize the purpose behind the artistic evaluation, the benefits can make a marked difference in the acceleration of the artist's career development.

Artist Evaluation

The first level of inquiry by the manager should be a personal assessment of the artist. The same general types of questions will apply to both individuals and groups. He should consider such basic questions as those involving the particular talent of the artist. Is he a vocalist? Instrumentalist? Comic? In the case of a singer, does he have his own vocal style or does he sound like other well-known recording artists? Does the artist write his own songs or routines? If not, what are the sources of his material? How good is the material? Is it commercial? What about the physical appearance of the artist? What are his strong and weak physical characteristics? How old is he? How old does he appear to be? Does he photograph well? Does he move well on stage? Does he speak well? What about his wardrobe? Are there any unconscious annoying mannerisms? What does his overall stage appearance look like? What about his name? Does his name reflect his appearance and stage image?

These are the types of questions the manager will want to ask. Even though the answers to some might make the artist uncomfortable, they must be addressed. To do otherwise would amount to self-deception.

For example, if the artist is an aspiring singer/songwriter with a unique voice but poor material, both artist and manager must deal with this fact. To ignore it would, in effect, overlook a flaw that could keep the artist from acquiring a recording contract. In this case, the artist should make a conscious effort to develop his songwriting over the long run, while both he and the manager should begin seeking commercial material suitable to the artist's style from music publishers and other writers.

As another example, let's suppose that the artist has strong, handsome facial features but is slightly overweight, thereby affecting his image on stage. The manager should suggest that the artist adopt a weight-reduction program. Meanwhile, the artist should wear clothes on stage that would accentuate his height and camouflage the extra pounds.

The artist should be viewed as a total package by the manager. Both artist and manager should try to objectively determine the overall impression the artist makes on an audience and what image he projects. Even though an artist may seem to be weak in a vital area, this may work to his advantage by making him different or unique. A resourceful manager will recognize weaknesses or points of differentiation and make an effort to capitalize on them if possible or to disguise or hide them if necessary.

The next area of inquiry in the artistic evaluation should be the artistic background and history of the artist. The artist and manager will want to structure their career planning so as to take maximum advantage of the artist's past successes and experience. They'll also naturally want to avoid repeating past mistakes and failures. For this reason, it's necessary for the manager to know in detail the artist's past history from a professional as well as a personal standpoint. He needs to know not only what the artist has done in the past, both good and bad, but also why he did those things. Insight into psychological makeup and motivation can be very revealing to the manager in structuring a plan for career development and fulfillment that will be best suited to the background and personality of his artist. This need for total awareness of the artist again illustrates the sensitivity that's required of the manager and the delicate nature of the evaluation process.

Specific areas of information that should be dealt with include: the artist's present status and past history with regard to personal appearances, including type and amount of experience; a list of the artist's contacts with agents, promoters, and club owners; and present status of bookings. Negative as well as positive aspects of the artist's past and present situation should be candidly discussed.

All of this information is useful in helping the manager structure an immediate network of contacts and possible return engagements in the personal appearance area that could be turned into immediate income for the artist.

As with personal appearances, the same type of questions should be asked in the area of recording, beginning with a review of the artist's present status, i.e., producer, recorded material in the can, and the like, as well as past affiliations with record companies, producers, and record executives. Previously released material, sales and airplay history, and contacts with radio program directors and disc jockeys should also be thoroughly discussed and noted. The parties should touch on anything relevant to furthering the artist's career as a recording artist, ranging from a discussion of A & R (Artist and Repertoire) men who have previously expressed interest in the artist, to the degree of actual studio experience the artist possesses. In addition, the parties should review and critique all of the artist's previously recorded material, both released and unreleased, in order to determine what steps should be taken in this area.

As with personal appearances and recording, this process of evaluating the present status of the artist, as well as his past history, should be repeated in every substantive area relevant to the artist's career. Other possible subject areas include public relations, songwriting, music publishing, television and motion pictures, commercials, merchandising and endorsements, and other areas of professional interest to the artist.

The detailed information concerning the artist and his career that is compiled in the artistic evaluation should enable the manager to begin the formulation of the artist's image.

Image Formulation

"Image" refers to exactly how and in what manner the artist is perceived by the public. An artist's image will be a reflection of his goals, talent, and lifestyle. It will have a direct bearing on the type of material he records and performs;

the people to whom he appeals; his dress, speech, and actions; and his advertising and publicity. There isn't a single aspect of his career or even his personal life that his image won't affect. Because of the overriding importance of an artist's image, its formulation and development will be one of the first major considerations of management. A determination of the image is a necessary prerequisite to career planning. Generally, the image will be determined in light of the artist's goals, abilities, and resources, and the existing commercial setting. Management will begin to structure and formulate an image after an analysis of all the relevant factors pertaining to the artist that were brought out during the artistic evaluation.

Goals. There are a number of factors that should be considered by the artist and manager in formulating an image that is best suited to the individual artist. The primary consideration revolves around the goals of the artist. He must decide what direction he wants to go with his career. An artist's image would differ radically depending on whether he wanted to be a classical concert pianist or the lead singer in a hard rock band.

Aside from professional goals, the personal goals of an artist should also be considered. The artist should be comfortable with his image in order to effectively project and perpetuate it. Also, as a general rule, an artist's image must be consistent with his personal lifestyle for the sake of credibility with his fans. This will, of course, depend on the particular direction the artist chooses for his career.

Present Image. Aside from the artist's professional and personal goals, a major consideration is his existing image. The manager should ask the question, "How is my artist presently perceived by the public as well as by others in the entertainment industry?" If an artist is new or relatively unknown, this won't present a problem, because there's no established perception of that artist. However the problem can be more difficult for an established artist who wants to renew a slipping career by changing his image. He runs the risk, first of all, of alienating those fans that he already has. Then there's also the danger that a radical change simply won't be accepted by the public. This can be especially true of an artist long known for a particular style of recording or performing. Another example of an artist who is trying to change his image occurs when a performer known for recording novelty material tries to record more serious material. For these reasons, an artist and his manager should pay careful attention to formulation and development of image. Flexibility should be built-in to allow for shifts in direction or development of an artist's art or music that will be accepted by the public without alienating present fans.

Finding the Right Image. Beyond these major considerations, manager and artist must develop an image that will compliment the talent, appearance, and personality of the artist, while still being commercially viable. For instance, let's assume that an artist's looks and style are compatible with the image of an early 1960s Greenwich Village folksinger. Nonetheless, projecting and perpetuating such an image would obviously be a blunder if there's no substantial market for that particular style of music. This demonstrates the important role that recognition of commercial opportunity plays in the selection of the artist's image.

The artist should always try to be an innovator rather than a follower. There's always the danger that an artist will try to follow a trend, only to become passé when the trend is no longer popular. This is a danger when an artist ties his image so closely to a particular trend. By the same token, innovations can spell disaster for an artist's career if the attempt to be different is too far out of line with the mainstream. This is an area where manager and artist must follow their instincts and temper the image with enough flexibility to avoid getting caught in the trap of a trend shift. This means keeping abreast of the current scene and gradually changing the artist's music and style to stay ahead or at least keep pace with changing tastes in the entertainment business.

Because an image is so important to the success of an artist, the manager must constantly be aware of the various factors that comprise it. Its formulation, projection, and perpetuation will depend on the artist's recording style and sound, his selection of material; his songwriting; the content and style of his personal appearances; his mode and style of dress, speech, and appearance; the types of interviews he grants; the content and methods of advertising affecting him; the television and radio shows on which he appears; and even the way he conducts himself offstage. These are all components of image that must constantly be monitored, reviewed, and refined and kept consistent by the manager.

Charisma. Another consideration in formulating an effective, commercially viable image is the element of charisma. "Charisma" is best described as some exceptional quality or magnetic power generated by an individual which allows him to stand out in a crowd or draw followers or fans to him. Charismatic qualities are often intangible in nature, yet they can spell the difference between just another artist and a superstar.

Managers should try to distinguish their artists from others by developing or maximizing the charismatic characteristics they might possess. This may take many forms. For instance, if an artist is from a distinctive region of the country, such as parts of the Deep South or Texas, emphasizing this may create curiosity about the regional characteristics of the artist which might, in turn, result in increasing his appeal. The same principle can be used by artists from foreign countries or by artists that tour countries other than their own. Another example of a possible charismatic trait is a slight imperfection. Here a manager can use an apparent handicap, such as blindness or a scar, as an advantage. An alternative lifestyle also may furnish another form of charismatic appeal. An example would be a reclusive artist in hiding who refuses to be interviewed or photographed. An age-old method of creating charisma is creating sexual mystique. This is a commonly used technique in today's entertainment business. These are all examples of how a manager can focus on a certain characteristic of an artist and use it in his image formulation and projection.

A successful manager will carefully evaluate and coordinate all of the various elements we've discussed that affect the artist's image into a consistent and credible pattern. An artist's image should never be left to chance. Neglect in dealing with an artist's image creates the danger that the public might be confused as to who the artist is or what he's trying to do. Another possibility is that the artist may develop a bad public image as a result of unfavorable press or a distorted perception of him. The manager and artist should always be on guard to protect against this type of situation.

Projecting and Developing the Image
Once image is formulated, the next step is to project and develop that image. This can be done in a variety of ways. One of the most effective methods of image projection is through live personal appearances at concerts, clubs, or showcases. To insure that the proper image is being projected, a manager will want to insure that the artist is appearing in the right market at the right arena before the right audience, and that his dress, speech, actions, material, and on-stage performance reinforce the image that has been formulated. The same considerations are true with regard to television or motion picture appearances. For this reason, personal appearances must be accepted or rejected against a backdrop of "career" considerations, and not just on the basis of money. For instance, an appearance on an influential television program may be an excellent career move, even though the financial compensation is well below the artist's standard personal appearance price.

Another valuable and effective means of image projection is through advertising and publicity campaigns aimed at the consumer and trade press and media. Photographs, press releases, print advertising, interviews, and radio and television time buys should be carefully conceived and calculated to reflect the artist's image. The manager should coordinate all such campaigns with the record company, publicity agent, or others involved in such activities. Whenever possible, the manager should retain the contractual right to approve any advertising, publicity and artwork reflecting on his artist. Without this right of approval, it's possible for the manager to lose control of image management.

Aside from planned campaigns, the manager should develop an attractive and well-planned press kit to give to members of the press, agents, promoters, and others who inquire about the artist. This kit should contain at least two 8" x 10" (20 x 25 cm) glossy photographs of the artist, a professionally written biography, reviews, a copy of the artist's latest recording, and other pertinent information regarding the artist. This is a relatively inexpensive image projection tool that can be highly effective in presenting the artist in the most positive light possible.

Other image projection devices include the artist's recordings, merchandising campaigns, commercials, endorsements, song folios, fan clubs, newsletters, even word of mouth among an artist's fans. Any contact an artist has with the public, either personally or through record sales, print, or the electronic media, is a method of image projection. Maximizing the artist's exposure to the public in a positive manner while avoiding the dangers of overexposure will to a large degree depend on how skillful a manager is in projecting the artist's image. Much is at stake in terms of financial reward and career development and maintenance. Because of the vital role that image plays in career success, comprehensive image planning and projection is an absolute must for today's successful artist manager.

9.
The Career Plan

We've made reference to the career plan on numerous occasions in previous chapters. Now, in this chapter, we'll discuss the fundamental concepts of business and creative planning and some of the considerations in formulating the plan. All the preliminary discussions, negotiation of the management contract, business organization, artistic evaluation, and image formulation are undertaken with the objective of enhancing the successful completion of the career plan. The career plan is the artist's and manager's conception of what is necessary to attain success in the entertainment industry. In one of the earlier chapters, reference was made to a young group who was approached by a manager wanting to represent the act. This would-be manager was full of promises and illusions of great things. However, the group made a key mistake when they failed to ask that all important question, "How will you make us a success?" The career plan is the "how" to successful artist management. Management professionals will have an idea, game plan, or pattern they utilize in attempting to help achieve success for their clients. They're generally anxious to discuss such a plan with the artist because it's from this exchange of ideas that the manager determines exactly what his client is seeking and how to best attain it.

In order to fully understand the formulation of the career plan, it helps to be aware of the many components that are involved in its makeup. A key element to any plan is the planner. The personal characteristics of the planner are always reflected in the plan. Whether an individual sets high or low objectives in a plan is usually governed by his personal traits. Is he a success-oriented person or is he negative in his approach to life? Whether the planner is an enthusiastic, persistent, dedicated optimist, or a pessimist by nature will obviously affect the formulation and execution of the career plan. No matter how well-constructed a plan may be, it will encounter problems if the planner maintains a consistent negative attitude. Moreover, if the planner is a traditional quitter, the effectiveness of a good career plan may never be known due to lack of follow-through. For purposes of our discussion, the career planner is both the manager and artist. Therefore, the personalities of both are indeed important.

Analyzing the Planner
One of the first steps in the career-planning process is to learn about the planner. The preliminary exploratory conference, contract negotiation, the business and artistic evaluation, and other meetings and discussions obviously will give manager and artist an insight into each other's personalities. Both the artist and manager should conduct a self-examination into their own success chemistry. Each should ask, "Am I a positive-minded person? Do I totally believe in this artist-management relationship? What do I want from this relationship? What are my personal strengths and weaknesses?" This self-appraisal will assist the planner in formulating the career plan, or it may add new insight and perspective into an existing plan.

In order to be realistic and effective, the planner should have insight into his own motivations, fears, and overall success pattern. For instance, if both manager and artist are formulating the career plan, a better awareness of themselves may prevent one of them from objecting to the high goal aspirations advanced by the other, especially if either artist or manager, is conscious that his basic approach to planning is conservative. Consequently, the party with the more dominant success chemistry will avoid compromising his position merely because his planning partner has tendencies toward "fear of failure" that could be detrimental to both. Conversely, if one party finds through self-analysis that he sets goals too high, or is unrealistic in his objectives, this awareness may make it easier for him to accept more realistic goals recommended by the other party in the planning process. Planning can be done by either artist or manager alone if necessary. The artist without a manager will be forced to plan alone. Nevertheless, the same principles and concepts will apply.

Establishing Goals

Another element of the career plan is the goal. Goals are objectives of the artist's career. Goals may range from successfully performing the nightclub circuit, to charting a top-ten record, to earning $1,000,000 in a year. Goals vary depending on the peculiar circumstances, needs, and desires of the artist. Realistic, attainable goal selection is crucial to the success of the artist/manager relationship.

The process of goal setting is often complex. A goal should stimulate and motivate the artist toward a particular achievement. The career planner should avoid setting his sights too high, thus making the goal extremely difficult or impossible to achieve. Nor should he set the goal so low that it's quickly accomplished, consequently losing its motivational value. A happy medium must be reached. Effective goal selection requires much thought and consideration. Too many goals may further complicate the process. The career planner will have to study the feasibility of each desired goal and rank them according to priorities. By applying the principles of open discussion and honest self-evaluation, the proper goals can be selected.

The speed of goal accomplishment is another important element of the career plan. The planner must take into consideration unexpected events that could delay the scheduled accomplishment of certain objectives. A timetable for goal attainment must be constructed to match each particular goal realistically. It can't be too soon, thereby not allowing sufficient time for its accomplishment. Neither can it be too distant, thereby losing motivational impact.

To design a realistic timetable, goals should be staggered over long, short, and intermediate periods. A certain objective can be set for achievement in six months thereby giving the artist something to work for with immediate results. Another goal can be set to be reached in one year, and still another set for three to five years. All the goals, of course, should be designed to lead to some ultimate objective, but the short and intermediate objectives give the entire plan a logical stair-step effect. Although the timetable is different for each level of achievement, the overall design is interrelated to the ultimate goal.

Another interesting factor influencing goal selection and accomplishment is the psychological makeup of the planner. While we discussed the self-image of the planner earlier in this chapter, we are concerned here with the less obvious personal influences affecting the career-planning process. Some individuals have a fear of failure. Consequently, this fear may reveal itself in terms of easily attainable goals over a very short period. There are others who fear success. This fear is camouflaged by setting goals that are almost impossible to attain. These individuals do not have to worry about success, since their goal will never be accomplished. They have a built-in excuse. "I knew I couldn't reach that goal—it's just too high," or, "I would have succeeded, except. . . ."

Another important point is the psychological assistance goals give in achieving success. The fact that a goal exists, is a good way to start.Writing down the goals is even better. Periodic reading or repetition of the goal will imprint that objective in the subconscious. Thus, conscious actions, which are controlled by following the career plan, are complimented by these subconscious thoughts. This can be very helpful when things don't seem to be going well and self-doubt sets in. At this point, a positive subconscious can help put an artist back on the route toward his goal.

Deciding on a Goal Strategy

Once a realistic goal has been selected, the next step is developing an approach for reaching that goal. We'll refer to these approaches as "goal strategies." The goal strategy is the planner's idea of the shortest, most effective route to a particular point, the goal. The artist's manager should realize that the goal strategies will almost always differ from artist to artist, depending on his particular talent, needs, and circumstances. A planner's selection of a particular goal will depend on how he views the career plan. His past experience, personal motivation, expertise, knowledge of the overall structure of the entertainment industry, and his sense of timing all play an important part in strategy selection. For instance, many artists wish to break into the national concert market. Several strategies could be employed to accomplish this goal. The artist could work on recording with hopes of selling his material to a record company, resulting in a chart record that would lead him into concerts. Alternatively, the artist could attempt to secure bookings as an opening act for an established concert headliner while working on the recording phase of his career. Still another approach would be for the artist to record and release his records through a small regional label with hopes of developing a market in that area as a concert attraction through local record sales, consequently attracting attention from a major label or national agents.

All these strategies could ultimately achieve the desired result. The pivotal question for management is, "Which strategy will be the most desirable for my particular artist?" The answer to this will be determined by the artist, his desires, motivations, personal characteristics, circumstances, and his career plan timetable.

Strategies are the pathways to goal attainment. They may be designed to follow just one route, or change directions on numerous occasions throughout the artist's career. Nonetheless, they should all lead in the same direction—toward the artist's goal.

Developing Career Tactics

The final step to career planning is developing career tactics. Once the goal is established and a strategy selected, daily movement toward accomplishing the objective must be planned. We'll call this daily achievement "career tactics." Career strategies set the direction toward particular goals, while career tactics are the actual moves of the strategy. They're the day-to-day activities of an artist's life. These seemingly unimportant activities may account for a month's or even a year's work toward the accomplishment of certain goals. The control of these activities is a critical aspect of goal achievement. Many people enjoy the talking, planning, and dreaming phase of planning. But the tactical phase isn't concerned with tomorrow; its concern is today. The manager and artist should personally ask what's being done right now toward accomplishing the predetermined career goals. It's at this point in the career plan where many lose control of their future. The future is controlled by the amount of time leading up to it. If a successful future is wanted, start with being a success today. To have high aspirations and to succeed takes hard work. To work efficiently and consistently takes discipline. Daily tactics inject discipline in the career plan.

Another factor associated with the overall career planning process is the planner's ability to efficiently utilize his time. Because of the rapid fluctuations in popular trends and styles in the entertainment business, time is of the utmost importance to the artist and manager. The artist who has achieved success must maximize his position before a new style emerges that may divert his following to a new rising star. The style that brought the artist to the peak of his career could be the very thing that leads to his demise. However, once an artist has achieved success, he's in a position to maximize and prolong his career if he works diligently. Efficiency is the key. Too many artists think that once they have a hit record, the work is over and the fun begins. It's not so—not if an artist wants to last. The artist, and especially the young artist, must be aware of the costs associated with the business. Studio rental fees, union stage hands, sidemen for recording, album cover art design, concert halls, and on and on. Working efficiently means knowing how to control such costs. This is to a great extent accomplished by controlling time. The artist's awareness and desire to maintain control over his time leads to efficiency. Efficiency leads to profit.

A final point: once the goal career, strategies, and tactics have been determined, the plan should be reviewed periodically. A review enables the planner to gauge results and to determine if a tactical or strategical change is necessary.

Often you hear an artist or manager comment, "How did that record make the charts?" or, "How could that artist be successful?" Here you should look behind the record or artist to the people planning the career. The success of the record or artist may become more apparent. Determined, positive-minded people with a well-thought-out, realistic career plan can greatly affect their prospects for success. They know where they're going and how they're going to get there. This is the essence of the career-planning concept.

10.
The Career Plan
In Action

To tie all the career planning concepts together, let's take the hypothetical example of the development of four young artists known as London Smile and their manager, Paul Chaffey. After a lengthy preliminary exploratory conference and several meetings, London Smile and Paul decide that they're right for each other. They want to enter into an artist-manager relationship. Paul seeks the counsel of an entertainment attorney who drafts the management agreement that is subsequently presented to the group. Since none of the members knows anything about the management agreement, they seek the advice of a local attorney, who also doesn't know anything about such agreements. However, the local attorney does have the presence of mind to contact an attorney in Nashville who specializes in entertainment law. Although London Smile and Paul have already agreed to the major points, their attorneys uncover some considerations that were overlooked. After several give and take sessions and consultations with their respective clients, the attorneys are able to work out these points to everyone's satisfaction. The management agreement is signed shortly thereafter. Paul Chaffey now has a client and London Smile a manager. Both are happy with the relationship and eager to begin work.

Paul immediately sets out to thoroughly examine the business organization of the group. He learns that all the members of London Smile are receiving the same pay and own all of the group's assets equally (consisting of a sound system and station wagon). After discussing the business organization of London Smile with their attorney, a recommendation is made that the group form a formal partnership. Following this advice, Paul discusses the matter with the members of the group. During this conversation, the topic changes from business to artistic goals. It's quite obvious from the discussion and the information gathered in the preliminary exploratory conference that one member, Craig Jones, is not as positive of his direction as the other members. After Paul explains the legal relationship of co-partners, Craig has additional doubts, especially since it would be necessary for the group to borrow substantial amounts to purchase equipment, wardrobe, and vehicles. While Craig is unsure about the group's direction and his legal relationship to the other members, he agrees that it's necessary to borrow the money for the purchase of the items they need. After much thought and discussion among all the members, Paul offers Craig an employment agreement whereby he'll receive a guaranteed fixed salary from London Smile. By accepting the employment agreement, Craig can still participate in the group (although not having a vote), without being tied down legally and financially to the partnership. Craig is very happy with this relationship. He can continue to develop himself artistically with a good group and manager, but without any long-term commitment to a situation that he's not as strongly committed to as the other members.

The group enters into an Articles of Partnership and subsequently signs an Employment Agreement with Craig Jones. London Smile is now a formal partnership. Next, Paul arranges a meeting with a local banker for the group's partners to discuss their financial needs. After several meetings, the banker is impressed with the partners, manager, and organized manner in which they conduct their business. He consents to make the loan for the various items they need to expand the group. However, the banker does have one request that Paul doesn't appreciate. He wants Paul to co-sign the note with the partners, since the loan is for a substantial sum and bank policy is somewhat vague concerning loans to entertainers. Knowing the obvious shortcomings of co-signing with the artists, Paul still agrees to do so. In addition, the banker asks for insurance coverage on all the new equipment being purchased with the loan proceeds, since it's being used as partial collateral for the loan. Key-man life insurance is also requested as additional protection. This proves to be no problem, since Paul has already anticipated these requests and has made arrangements with an experienced insurance agent. The day the loan is closed, the group opens a checking account at the bank. They're excited about purchasing the needed equipment. Their future looks bright. Craig Jones is also relieved that he doesn't have to sign the large bank note. To make life even better, he also receives his first paycheck from the group.

Paul has an attorney file the group's name for service-mark protection and retains an accountant to set up a simple set of accounting records for the group. A budget is prepared using last year's earnings, coupled with a forecast of current year's income based on new markets that the group's expansion will hopefully capture. Paul feels the group's business is organized and in a healthy condition. He can now turn his attention to the artistic evaluation of London Smile.

During the preliminary exploratory conference phase, Paul has become quite familiar with the group's strengths and weaknesses. He knows the good as well as the bad with regard to each member's individual characteristics. While Craig Jones is one of the better singers in the group, Paul realizes that there's a potential image problem. Craig wants to be a front man. The other members want London Smile to develop as a group. This disagreement over image is probably the primary reason Craig doesn't want to become a partner. So Paul decides to use the abilities of all members to the utmost. He'll capitalize on Craig's talent while encouraging the other members to develop their ability. Fortunately, the group looks good on stage and has developed a strong following in the local club and college markets. They're a poised, live performance act. While Craig is still the front man, the band is being perceived by their audiences as a group, not as a single artist with a band. Unfortunately, however, the group has had no recording experience. They're further limited by the fact that no one in the group writes original material. Paul's creative assessment uncovers several good aspects of the group, but as is the case with any new act, he also finds many shortcomings.

After obtaining information during the preliminary exploratory conference, the business planning stage, and the creative assessment phase, Paul knows what London Smile wants—a top-ten record. Their goal is easy to identify. But its accomplishment will be somewhat more difficult. Realizing the improbability of this occurrence, Paul recommends that the group set their goal in three phases. The overall goal will be just what they want, a top-ten record—but in three years, not one.

As an intermediate goal (within one year), the group will shoot for four good recordings. As a short-run objective (within six months), the group will concentrate on locating original songs to record that will be suitable to their style.

During the next six months, Paul and the group work diligently at finding original material to record. Paul contacts music publishers regarding unrecorded material that will be suitable to the style of his clients. All the group members listen to original material of songwriter friends and other artists. Also during this time, Paul negotiates the best studio rental deal possible for the upcoming sessions. Fortunately, the group's engagements are taking care of themselves through local agency contacts the group had established before entering into the management agreement with Paul. The new equipment, wardrobe, vehicles, and fresh enthusiasm seem to make the group more professional. This professionalism pays off in audience acceptance and consequently in more dates for better money.

As scheduled, the group finds several original compositions they like. The songs are well-rehearsed and, within the year, the group records the material. Upon completing the session, Paul and the group are absolutely "knocked out" with their recordings. In their opinion, they're all hits. Paul enthusiastically announces he'll leave for Los Angeles within the week to "shop" the tapes.

Shortly thereafter, Paul returns from Los Angeles totally depressed. He's unable to see most A & R men at the record companies. The ones that do hear London Smile's material aren't impressed. While the A & R men comment that the recordings were not necessarily bad, they don't think there's anything distinctive about them. Needless to say, the group is disappointed with Paul's reports. All agree that during the next year (the second year of the management agreement) more emphasis will have to be put on recording. They decide to keep the same three-year objective and select new six-month and one-year goals. They'll keep the best two songs from the previous recordings and continue to look for new material. By the end of the six months, they want to have a total of ten original songs to record. They all agree that the new recording sessions will take more time than the previous ones. One of the members has become totally disgusted with the material being submitted by publishers and other artists and starts writing for the group. Although his first compositions aren't that good, he does show promise. Within six months, the new material has been gathered, and before the year is up, the group completes recording the eight new songs, plus re-recording the two best songs from the previous recordings. They're astonished at how much better the new recordings are compared to the first.

Paul anxiously schedules another trip to Los Angeles. After three days of attempting to see A & R men and listening to critical comments from the ones who will listen to his tapes, Paul is contemplating a change of profession. He starts harboring thoughts of self-doubt about himself as a manager. Why can't he make a deal? Is it him? Or, is it true what the A & R men are saying, that the group doesn't have a unique style? The recordings aren't as clean as they could be. The mix is poor. The vocal performance doesn't fit the material. The long flight home gives Paul time to think and recover from his overwhelming disappointment. He analyzes the failure of his attempt to get London Smile a record deal. Paul asks himself the question, "Why did we fail?" He then lists all the negative comments and suggestions from the various A & R men. After studying their input, he does find some similarity in their comments.

Next Paul tries to make a list of all the good things that come out of the trip. There are two. He's able to see more A & R men on this trip than the last. And, the record people he talks to during the trip seem to take more time with him and offer some genuine criticism, coupled with ideas for improvement. One even gives him the name of a producer who he thinks could help the group. By the time Paul arrives home, he's pulled himself together. He reports his disappointing findings to the group, but also stresses the positive aspects of the trip. Based on this fresh information, Paul announces a new plan for year three of the management agreement. He recommends that the group devote a substantial portion of its time in the next year to recording. By doing this, the number of live performances London Smile is playing will have to be reduced, consequently, reducing the group's income. The partners of the group will ultimately bear the loss of income in terms of reduced partner draws. But, Paul feels that if recording is the route to success for London Smile, this aspect of their career has to be accelerated.

All of the partners except one agree with Paul. The one dissenting partner argues that he can't make it on a reduced salary. The amount he's receiving now isn't enough to support his family. A reduced salary will put him in an impossible situation. He'll have to leave the group. Paul and the remaining partners are sympathetic to his argument, but what can they do? The group is experiencing its first real crisis.

After weighing the alternatives of keeping the dissenting partner and not increasing their recording output, or following through with the new plan, the other partners decide to accept Paul's plan, regardless of the consequences. The dissenting partner agrees to stay with the group until they find a replacement, which they do within a month. The old partnership is dissolved and a new one formed with the remaining two members. The replacement for the departing partner is hired as an employee. The new member accepts the job at a salary far less than anyone else is making since he's young and has no major financial responsibilities. The fact that London Smile is going to put so much emphasis on recording is another reason the new member takes the job at a low starting salary.

Six weeks later the crisis has been overcome. Everyone is happy again and eager to get started on the new plan. Craig Jones is especially pleased since he didn't have to get involved with all the personnel problems, and he's still receiving his weekly check.

Paul sets out to get the new plan in motion. He contacts the producer recommended by one of the A & R men. Surprisingly, the producer has heard of the group and is interested in working on their new project.

Paul's strategy is to accelerate recording and close a deal with a record company by the end of the year. From a tactical standpoint, the group is aiming to complete twenty sides during the year. After many hours of work, London Smile accomplishes its objective. By the end of the year, the group has twenty new recordings in the can. While impressed with their work, the group is cautiously optimistic. The producer who has worked with them says he'll do all in his power to help them get a deal. Paul takes the three best recordings back to the A & R man who had shown interest by recommending the producer. The A & R man is impressed; however, he thinks the recordings need sweetner (strings and background voices.). However, he informs Paul that his company will pay the costs to have this done. Within the month, the requested changes are made. Shortly thereafter, the A & R man and Paul do strike a deal. London Smile is signed to a major record company, and within the year, as planned.

The group's objective always remained the same—a top-ten record. In this case, the strategical approach remains fairly constant since the manager and group feel that recording was the most direct route. Now that London Smile has secured a record deal, their strategy will change.

Emphasis now has to be placed on developing a unique concert presentation and obtaining a major booking- agency relationship. Their public relations image will have to be perfected. Paul and his clients set out to plan the next phase of London Smile's career, just like the earlier stages.

Summary

The story of Paul Chaffey and London Smile is entirely hypothetical, but throughout the story, many of the planning theories and practices we've discussed earlier are displayed. While the group went through considerable disappointment, personnel turnover, and financial setback, the key members still persisted. The outcome of the story could have been changed for the worse at any step of the way by introducing a new circumstance, such as partners who lacked a determined attitude, inexperienced management, failure of the group to follow through with its plan, and so on. While the group didn't achieve its ultimate goal, a top-ten record, they made enough progress toward its accomplishment to know that it was attainable. London Smile and Paul Chaffey are to be congratulated for getting the record deal they wanted. Their degree and length of success will depend on the same discipline that got them this far. The work, worry, and problem-solving is certainly not over. There'll be more crises to overcome. But we think Paul and London Smile will make it.

Part III
Making the
Plan Work

11.
Making Your
Own Breaks

Talent, organization, and planning are all essential elements of a successful career in show business. However, unless an artist's talent receives the proper exposure or unless the career plan is implemented, the artist is no better off than he was before he initiated his management program.

Making the plan work is the key to success for any artist. It can also be the most demanding part of a manager's job. It requires daily attention to detail and constant follow up. It means creating opportunities, making things happen, and turning dreams into reality. This is where a manager can be an invaluable asset to his artist.

For the new artist, the implementation or "break-in" phase probably represents the most difficult and frustrating stage of his career. The commitment of the artist and his manager is tested severely. It requires a tremendous amount of persistence, drive, and skill to cope with the inevitable obstacles that stand between an unknown artist and his ultimate goal of stardom. Many talented performers and their managers are not equipped financially or emotionally for the "dues paying" that is associated with this phase of the artist's career. As a result, many artists who receive initial rejections from agents, producers, and record companies become discouraged and quit. Artists and their managers should prepare themselves for this type of rejection and resolve not to let it get the best of them. Success comes to those capable of rising above this type of adversity. Those who can't will never make it.

Even artists who do enjoy a measure of recognition and financial reward soon learn that success is relative. There's always the potential that hard-earned success might disappear as quickly as it materializes. Every artist is only as successful as his most recent accomplishment. He quickly discovers that to maintain his level of achievement requires continuous planning, execution, and follow through. The competition for the limited number of slots on the charts is fierce. Unless the artist and his management are aware of this, they'll soon find themselves being "has beens." This suggests that implementation and execution of the career plan is a never-ending process.

This chapter and the ones that follow are designed to acquaint the manager and artist with the specific problems that they'll undoubtedly face in implementing their plans. They also suggest approaches and techniques for understanding and effectively dealing with these problems. While every manager develops his own techniques and approaches for achieving the goals of the artist, we feel that the information and advice contained in this section will serve as a good foundation for helping him adopt an effective implementative program.

Ingredients for Success
Successfully implementing the many aspects of an artist's career plan involves the interaction of a number of factors.

The Artist. The first variable is the artist. Unless the artist possesses at least some degree of talent and appeal, the most experienced manager, working with the best plan conceivable, won't succeed in making that artist successful. The ultimate decisionmaker is the general public, not the manager. It's the public who will ultimately accept or reject the artist, based on what they hear and see.

The Manager. While the manager can't insure success, he does have a great deal to say about how the artist presents his talent to the public, as well as the type and degree of exposure he receives. Record charts and motion picture box-office receipts bear witness to the fact that persons of only average or less than average ability have achieved stardom through astute, effective management.

Knowledge and understanding of the various aspects of the entertainment industry are essential prerequisites for any manager. Unless a manager possesses a working knowledge of the particular field of entertainment in which his artist is involved and is able to function effectively within it, he's of little use to his client. This knowledge and understanding takes many forms. Every manager should know the mechanics of the particular area in which he's involved, whether it be recording, publishing, performing, merchandising, motion pictures, television, theater, and so on. This means knowing the inner workings of each, knowing what the prevailing industry practices are, and having the ability to speak the language of that particular aspect of the business. It's also essential that the manager know the decisionmakers within each branch of the industry, or at least know who they are. The entertainment business is a "people business." Personal contacts can mean everything when it comes to getting a deal for an unknown artist or arranging the "right" exposure for him. Many recording executives, agents, publishers, and motion picture and television executives depend on word-of-mouth reports or personal recommendations concerning new or unproven artists, writers, and actors. This is a necessity because so many amateurs and thrillseekers are drawn to show business by the promise of glamour and wealth. Entertainment executives are constantly hounded by these types of people. As a result, they must depend on their personal contacts with established managers, proven artists, and other industry executives for referrals and tips to insure that they deal with professionals. While this attribute of the industry is often criticized by new artists and many managers, professionals view it as a necessary self-defense mechanism.

Consequently, for a manager to pierce this protective shield and present his artist to an entertainment decision-maker, it's often necessary that the manager "know" someone. Like it or not, it's a reality of the business.

It's clear that knowledge of the industry and personal contacts are necessary tools of any effective manager. However, the truly successful manager possesses the intangible quality of "having a feel for the business." This is a combination of perception, understanding, judgment, and timing. It means knowing how to calm a temperamental artist or communicate a certain mood to a studio musician. Having a feel for the business also means understanding the subtle business and personal interrelationships that exist in the various components that make up the entertainment industry.

An illustration of this intangible ability is an accurate prediction by a manager of how a certain television appearance by an artist will affect that artist's concert following and record sales. Another example is the ability of a manager to sense under-exposure or over-exposure of his artist by reviewing his itinerary three months ahead of time and adjusting accordingly. All top-flight managers have this keen ability of making the right move at the right time.

"How do I acquire these essential management tools?" This is a question asked by every aspiring manager breaking into the field. Books such as this one can help acquaint the new manager and artist with management concepts and the structure of the entertainment industry. Weekly trade magazines are published to keep a manager informed of current happenings and trends in the business. These two sources are highly recommended. However, books and trade publications can't establish personal contacts for the manager or provide him with the ingredients of understanding the business. Actual experience in some aspect of entertainment, regardless of the specific area of the business, is the only means available to the aspiring manager to provide the artist with the necessary insight and feel for this unique profession. Practical experience also affords him the opportunity to meet others in the business. The entertainment industry is relatively small. Business decisionmaking is concentrated primarily in a few entertainment centers, such as New York, Los Angeles, and Nashville. For these reasons, it's possible to meet a wide cross-section of entertainment industry figures by working and living in an entertainment center. Because entertainment is a small industry and people advance themselves by accumulating practical experience, chances are good that a friend who's struggling today might be one of tomorrow's top decisionmakers.

Preparation. Preparation by the artist and manager is another necessary ingredient for success. Planning is one form of preparation already discussed. Always being ready to carry out that plan is another aspect of preparation. Show business is unpredictable. Opportunity often knocks when least expected. Both artist and manager must always be in a position to capitalize on a "break" when it appears, because it might not present itself again. This means that both should know exactly where they want to go and how they expect to get there, and have the ability to back it up.

So many of today's stars attribute their success to being able to take advantage of an opportunity. These brief and often chance events are the best reasons for constant preparation, planning, and rehearsal. If the artist and manager are "ready," it will be just a matter of doing what both have prepared themselves for when the right opportunity presents itself.

Attitude. Flexibility and a realistic approach go hand-in-hand with preparation. The artist and manager should always be willing to change the game plan to fit the circumstances. Trends in entertainment can change overnight. Being able to anticipate and change with them is essential to achieving and maintaining success. Elvis Presley, through the efforts of astute management, sustained and expanded his career through three decades. By being able to remain flexible, Elvis made the transition from rock 'n roll recording idol to movie star to Las Vegas headliner.

Flexibility is not only important for the established artist but applies equally to the new artist in the break-in stage. The unknown artist must constantly adapt to meet existing commercial opportunity. What might have been in vogue a year ago means nothing if the public won't accept it today.

Being realistic is an attitude that must be maintained by artist—the struggling unknown artist as well as the established superstar—and manager alike. Entertainment lends itself to big promises that have a way of never materializing and to firm commitments that often dissolve into maybes. Part of the manager's job is to sort through these promises, offers, and alternatives and make a realistic assessment of the value of each. He must help maintain a realistic perspective on the artist's part while at the same time sustaining his own enthusiasm and commitment as well as that of his artist. This requires an ability to recognize a true commercial opportunity and take steps to turn it to the artist's advantage. It also means rejecting offers that may look good on the surface but turn out to have little real merit. It's often difficult to effectively perform this function, especially in light of the many glamour offers that "can't miss." However, unless the manager can retain his perspective and make accurate judgments, the chances of his artist making it to the top and staying there are slim.

As mentioned earlier in the chapter, persistence and determination, in addition to everything else, are in many ways the most important qualities to be possessed by anyone who seriously intends a career in show business. The ability to accept disappointment and setbacks without giving up marks the difference between stars and ordinary people with talent.

This type of single-purpose drive is necessary not only to unknowns, but to established artists as well. One of the best examples is recording-artist Kenny Rogers who enjoyed a hit record in the late 1950s as a single artist. After that early success, he faded from the charts. He later came back with a new group, the "First Edition," which enjoyed a string of hit records throughout the late '60s and early '70s. After what seemed to be a period where success was guaranteed, another dry-spell hit. The group broke up and Kenny moved to Nashville and began recording country-oriented material. After a couple of years absence from the charts, he enjoyed another comeback, recording the biggest hits of his career. The underlying reason for this success is that Kenny never gave up. He was determined to find a new approach that would put him back on the charts, not just once, but twice.

This type of roller-coaster effect is typical of a show business career. The artist and manager should realize this from the outset. If the talent is there and the commitment is strong enough, something will usually happen sooner or later. The time in between is for paying dues. This is something both artist and manager should be prepared to do if they really want to make it.

All of the qualities described in this chapter can at least to some extent be controlled by the artist and his manager; however, there's one element that can't. That element is luck.

Luck. Luck is as much a part of entertainment as talent. Simply stated, luck is being in the right place at the right time. There are many artists who have been in the right place at the right time but were not properly prepared to make the most of the opportunity. Doing this is the essence of making your own breaks. Although a good manager can't make a lucky break materialize, he can help create the circumstances of commercial opportunity through his knowledge, contacts, and understanding of the industry. He can through preparation, flexibility, and realism help insure that his artist will be ready to take advantage of that opportunity he has helped to create. This is what successful artist management is all about—helping the artist to make his own breaks, rather than leaving success to chance. This is the difference between an artist sitting back waiting for a break that may never come and an artist with a well-planned and executed management program designed to make sure that the break will come sooner or later.

12.
The Artist's Development Team

Previous chapters have dealt with the importance of organization, planning, and affirmative action by the artist and manager to help create commercial opportunity. At this point, we'd like to introduce the concept of the artist's development team and its role in the career success of the artist.

What is The Artist's Development Team?

The term "artist's development team" refers to the various entities or people within the entertainment industry who have a direct monetary interest or stake in the artist's career and with whom the manager and artist must deal on an ongoing basis. For instance, let's assume the artist's income is derived primarily from the sale of records, songwriting royalties, personal appearances, and commercial endorsements. Those entities or persons who stand to directly benefit from the artist's success would include his record company, music publisher, booking agent, and advertising agency. These entities comprise the artist's development team.

Each of these entities is vitally concerned that the artist succeed because its success is tied, at least in part, to that artist. Each member of the team has certain resources and assets he's willing to expend in order to further various aspects of the artist's career. Any experienced manager knows that without the help of these various entities, career development toward the artist's predetermined goals would be almost impossible. By the same token, maximizing the contributions of each member of the team in a coordinated, efficient manner consistent with the artist's career plan can insure that those goals are attained. As a result, everyone benefits.

The Principle Behind the Artist's Development Team

The concept of the artist's development team shows recognition of a very basic principle of the entertainment industry: No one can ever hope to achieve success alone. The most resourceful manager, working with the best plan conceivable and the most talented artist imaginable, also must have the support and help of others within the industry in order to make it.

With this basic principle in mind, the manager should strive to maximize the career development of his artist by working with the various members of the team for the mutual success of all involved. Through a program of coordinated interplay with the artist and the respective team members, the manager should be able to accelerate the career plan. This is accomplished by obtaining the maximum benefits that may be derived from proper allocation of each team member's expertise and resources.

The concept of an artist's development team is by its very nature a positive approach. To apply it successfully, the manager must necessarily establish harmonious, cooperative working relationships with those individuals who make up the team. This requires the manager to be an open-minded, cooperative person who is willing to listen to the recommendations and suggestions of others. This is not to suggest he be just a follower. He must know where his artist is going and set the pace for others.

Before going any further, it should be understood that this basic management approach does not ignore the manager's responsibility to assert and protect the artist's rights when necessary. However, a successful application of this approach should allow the manager to maximize the benefits to be derived for his artist without having to compromise his rights or artistic integrity.

We're realistic enough to acknowledge that disputes between team members and management are sure to arise during the career of any artist. But the role of management is to shield the artist from such disputes as much as possible, while making an effort to resolve these conflicts through compromise or alternative approaches. Under the artist's development team approach, the manager should try to minimize points of disagreement when they arise so they don't impede the progress of career development any more than necessary.

While disagreements are inevitable, especially in a creative industry where personal taste and preference plays such an important part in decision-making, many needless disputes could be avoided. Most avoidable disputes arise as a result of ego. A manager should remember that he's working to build his artist's career, not to gratify his own self-image. Use of the manager's sense of self-discipline and pragmatism is very important in avoiding these types of petty, time-consuming disagreements. By the same token, the manager's ability to communicate and counsel his client can help avoid artist-related ego hangups. One helpful device for avoiding these types of problems is for the manager and artist to recognize and weigh the counterproductive effects of such disputes against the benefits that can be derived and the progress that could be made if a given dispute didn't occur. By consciously making this assessment, both manager and artist will often realize that the dispute is simply not as important as they originally thought it was. Many artists and managers waste much valuable time and energy on trivial, unimportant problems. Eventually through experience the rational pragmatist will learn how to avoid this.

While a realistic, resourceful manager can help avoid creating his own problems, unless he recognizes that he won't necessarily be as successful with someone else's problems, this situation is bound to cause ego-related snags. The best approach to problem-solving is for the manager to try to negotiate a solution without compromising the artist. This often means that the manager must swallow his pride to achieve the desired results. Another tack he may take is to approach a problem from a different perspective or provide the other party with alternatives. In any event, he must remain cool and keep the lines of communication open. By doing this, a manager will find himself winning far more times than he loses.

Forming the Team

With the concept of the artist's development team in mind, the next question the manager should be asking is, "Exactly how do I go about dealing with the artist's development team?"

The first step is to identify the team members or potential team members. For example, if the artist is presently affiliated with a record company and a music publisher but not a booking agent, the former two companies would be team members, while any of a number of booking agents would be potential team members. The manager's next move would be to secure affiliation with an agent or agents to fill the vacancy on the team. He'd seek to add other members to the team based on the overall career plan and needs of the artist. Other possible team members might be a record producer, publicity firm, television producer, and so forth. Members of the team will often be added or dropped, depending on their involvement with the artist at any given point in his career.

Establishing Personal Relationships with Team Members

Once the various entities comprising the team are identified or essential members subsequently added, the manager should personally get acquainted with every individual that will have a role in the development of the artist's career. We stress the importance of "every" person who has a contribution to make, not just the president of the record company or the responsible agent in charge of booking the artist. This means getting to know the personnel comprising each respective department at the record label from the president to the secretaries. With regard to the booking agency, this means taking the time to meet and get to know not only the agent primarily responsible for booking the artist, but his assistant as well as other agents and supporting personnel in other departments.

Besides just getting acquainted, the manager should tell these people about his artist, what he is doing artistically and where he is trying to go with his career. This will help the team members to better understand the artist on whose career they will be working to help develop. A better understanding can be the beginning of genuine excitement and belief in the artist and his art.

The truly successful manager takes the extra time to establish personal relationships with as many people as he can on a one-to-one basis. It makes a difference when it comes time to getting things done or having quick access to information. Everyone involved with the artist, regardless of his or her specific duties, has a contribution to make to the artist's career. It's human nature for these people to give a little extra or be a little more responsive or cooperative when they are dealing with a manager they know on a personal level. People appreciate being appreciated. They like knowing the manager thinks their input is worthwhile. The difference will show up in the success of the artist's career.

It's often a good idea, depending on the particular situation, to introduce the artist to various team members. This personal contact helps to make their efforts more meaningful while also allowing them a greater depth of understanding about the artist.

Coordinating the Team's Activities

A managerial prerequisite to effectively dealing with the artist's development team is a detailed comprehension of the structure, role, and function of each component of the team. In short, this means that the manager should understand the workings of the record industry, booking agencies, promoters, music publishing, television, merchandising, commercials, and endorsements, and how each segment relates to the other.

The most frequent criticism of managers by record company executives, producers, agents, and publishers is that they often don't understand the various aspects of the entertainment business. As a result, they're unprepared to work effectively with the various members of the artist's development team to further their client's career. As pointed out earlier, this knowledge is absolutely essential to an artist's long-term success.

As mentioned in the preceding chapter, there's no quick way to fully understand the entertainment industry. Practical experience is the best teacher. Unless the manager has the proper background and experience, he'd be ill advised to undertake the management of an artist's career in the first place. There's a great danger that an inexperienced manager representing a promising artist will be unprepared to fully develop his artist's career. If he doesn't know how to deal knowledgeably and effectively with every component of the artist's development team, he could irreparably damage his client's career.

Even if the artist's career has sufficient momentum to overcome managerial inexperience at this stage, lack of competence and expertise could result in more serious long-range problems for both the manager and artist. Once a manager is labeled an incompetent or amateur by other industry professionals, his chances of regaining their esteem are slim. This will not only involve his future effectiveness within the industry, but also will reflect on his artist's prospects for achieving maximum career fulfillment. For this reason, we feel that it's critical that the manager have the knowledge and experience to accept and deal effectively with the demanding challenges of managing a career at the artist's development team level. Like the artist, the manager must be ready to respond effectively when opportunity knocks.

After the members of the team have been identified, personal relationships are in various stages of development, and the manager is sufficiently prepared by knowledge and experience to deal effectively with the team, the actual process of artist development should begin.

The manager should strive to maximize the resources available to his artist from the various components of the artist's development team. To do this, the manager must necessarily help each team member achieve his own special goals while insuring that those individual goals are beneficial to and consistent with the artist's overall career goals. This requires a high degree of coordination and communication with each team component to insure that everybody is pulling toward the same objective in a manner that will compliment the plans and actions of all other team members. For instance, the manager will want to insure that an extensive personal appearance tour is timed to maximize the promotion of the artist's latest record release. This requires coordination and communication between the marketing, advertising, publicity, and promotion departments of the record company, and the artist's booking agency. If the manager can effectively serve as the liaison between these two team members, he can help each to realize their specific goals. The personal appearance will reinforce the company's promotional efforts, thereby resulting in increased record sales for the company. Because of the new record release, there's increased interest in the artist, thus making him more appealing to promoters. This, in turn, makes the agent's job easier in booking the tour. In this example, management's coordination efforts make it possible for both team members to achieve their particular goals. The artist benefits from royalties linked to the record sales and the income from the personal appearance.

To be effective in this area, the manager must maintain constant communication with various development team members. He should keep them informed of the artist's activities and plans. He should also monitor the plans and desires of the various team members. The manager should remember that he's the focal point for all information concerning the artist and all communication between the team members and the artist. The manager should make himself readily available to representatives of the various team members.

In addition to controlling the information and communication functions, the manager should try to anticipate the specific goals of the various team members. For example, by anticipating the direction that the record company wants to go with an artist, the manager can plan accordingly. If he agrees with the direction, he can arrange the artist's schedule to coincide with those plans so as to gain maximum benefit from the record company. If he feels the company's plans don't fit into what he and the artist have determined to be the proper direction, he can propose alternatives or present his view of what should be the next move in a logical, persuasive manner before time pressures lead to a confrontation or a serious disagreement.

The manager should also make an effort to understand and appreciate the limitations and problems of the particular team members. By knowing what's possible and what's unrealistic, he can phrase his requests in such a manner that he can probably get what he wants. This is a means of maximizing support from the various team members for the benefit of the artist.

The resourceful manager will take the initiative in helping the various team members achieve their goals by submitting proposals and ideas. He should, whenever possible, act as a catalyst with the various team members. He should be careful not to appear to be telling someone else how to do their job or to be demanding that his ideas always be utilized. Rather, he should approach various individuals with suggestions and alternatives and ask for their views or opinions. This should be a cooperative process aimed at trying to give an individual team member the benefit of a different viewpoint or alternative from which to choose.

The artist's development team concept is one the manager must utilize according to his best judgment. Some individuals might feel this type of initiative is a criticism of their abilities or a threat to their egos. Some people prefer that managers not be so actively involved in their particular area of responsibility. The manager should respect the wishes of these individuals and treat them accordingly, provided the interests of his artist don't suffer as a result.

Summary
The bottom line to the artist's development team concept is that the manager should strive to deal as effectively and efficiently as possible with each individual concerned with the artist's career. Every manager will have his own particular techniques for getting the job done. These techniques will necessarily vary with each particular person with whom the manager deals. Common sense, flexibility, and follow up are the key words to remember.

Regardless of the approach used, the manager should remember that the more he contributes to helping the various development team members achieve their own success, the more he is contributing to the success of his artist.

13.
The Record Deal

A successful record company affiliation is the key to any career in the music industry. Besides being a potentially lucrative source of income, the record is the most effective career development tool the artist possesses. It allows him to reach millions of potential fans with his music. This translates not only into record sales but also demand for concert and television appearances, offers for merchandising and commercial work, and a basis for songwriting income. Every element of the artist's career revolves around his relationship with the record company.

Because of the importance of the record, competition for the relatively few places on a record company's roster is fierce. Record company A & R departments are swamped with new artists and their managers, producers, or attorneys who are trying to "get a deal." The president of a well-known major label told us that his office alone receives over a thousand submissions a year. Out of this number, he'll sign two or three new acts.

This chapter is designed to help familiarize the new artist and his manager with the recording aspect of the artist's career. This information, hopefully, will help them to achieve a successful record-company affiliation.

Making a Quality Recording

The first objective in the recording phase of the artist's career is to produce a commercial recording of professional quality. There are two approaches the artist can take. The first is to try to record a finished master recording that can be sold or leased to a record company. The other is to produce a high-quality demo (demonstration recording) that will create interest in the artist by a record label. There are pros and cons to both approaches.

The Finished Master Recording. A finished master recording is desirable from several standpoints. If the record company likes what they hear, the tape can be pressed and released in a short period of time. Some companies prefer to listen only to finished masters because they know what they're buying and won't be required to spend additional time and money on re-recording. This allows the company to concentrate on the marketing and promotional aspects of the record business.

A major negative factor to the finished master approach is the expense involved. Recording and mixing two finished sides can cost the artist several thousand dollars or more in studio time, tape cost, and musician payments. A finished master-quality album can cost as little as $10,000 to as much as the artist wants to spend. Another problem with this approach is that many new artists lack the recording experience necessary to turn out first-class commercial recordings in the early stages of their careers. A finished master makes it difficult to make changes a record company may want. As a result, the company may reject the recording entirely.

The Multi-Track Demo. An alternate approach is for the artist to record a quality multi-track demo that will give the record company a chance to listen to the artist's material and singing style. The company may make suggestions to improve the recording or suggest other material the artist could record. This approach allows the label to get involved at the outset of the artist's career as to every detail of the artist's recordings.

The problem with this approach is that some companies prefer not to commit the time needed to develop an artist from a recording standpoint. Rather, they prefer the artist be capable of recording a finished product before they'll offer a contract. Unless a demo is of professional quality and has a high degree of commercial potential, the record company may choose not to get involved with the artist. Signing an artist is a business decision. As a result, the companies are looking for the "sure thing" when they can get it. Since the demo isn't a finished product, the risk factor is increased for the company. As a result, the A & R department may choose not to get involved.

Finding a Producer

Regardless of the approach used, in order to turn out successful recordings, the artist must coordinate a number of factors. The first is to find a producer.

It's the job of the record producer to mold the elements of artist, song, arrangement, studio, engineer, and musicians into a finished product. Many experienced artists are producers themselves. Many others don't feel capable of performing this important function. Whether the artist attempts to fill the dual role of producer or retain the services of another, it's essential that someone be in charge of the recording process.

Choosing a producer is much like choosing a manager. They all have their own way of doing their job, but their methods aren't nearly as important as their results. The qualities an artist and manager should look for in a producer are experience, track record, and an ability to understand the musical direction of the artist and to work with him on a creative level. Often, the producer may be the artist himself, although the new artist is probably better advised to find someone with experience. In some cases, the manager may be qualified to serve this dual function. In other instances, the artist may retain the services of an experienced, independent record producer. Whatever the choice, artist, manager, and producer must be able to work closely with each other to help develop the artist's recording career in a manner that is consistent with the artist's ability, image, and career plan.

Contractually, there are two basic approaches to the artist-producer relationship.

The Exclusive Personal Services Agreement. One is for the artist to sign an exclusive personal services agreement with an independent producer who would be responsible for payment of a negotiated royalty to the artist. The producer would, in turn, seek a recording affiliation by offering himself and the artist to the company as a package. Under such an arrangement, the producer signs an agreement with the record company, who pays all advances and royalties directly to the producer, who in turn accounts to the artist.

A major advantage to this approach is that a well-known independent producer, through his contacts, may be able to make a deal that the artist or manager may not otherwise be capable of obtaining. In addition, the name value and experience of a hot producer can make a big difference in breaking a new artist once a deal is made.

The major disadvantage is that the artist is exclusively tied to the musical tastes, production style, and fortunes of the producer. If the producer encounters a cold streak, the artist doesn't have the option of looking elsewhere for recording guidance. If a disagreement arises between the label and the producer, the artist's career could suffer as a result.

The Producer-for-Hire Approach. The other alternative is for the artist to be signed directly to the record company. In this situation, the artist would employ a producer on a project-by-project basis for either a flat fee or percentage of the artist's royalties or a combination of both.

This approach is certainly preferable from the standpoint of giving the artist and manager more control over the recording aspect of the artist's career. The fortunes of the artist are not tied to one producer. However, the producer-for-hire approach is not always available to the new artist because of the expense involved and the inability of the artist to get a deal without the help of an independent producer.

Should the artist enter into an exclusive production agreement, he and his manager should try to limit the terms of the contract to provide for termination of the agreement in the event the relationship is no longer beneficial to the artist. This is a negotiable point and will depend on the bargaining positions of the parties.

After becoming familiar with the artist's ability, style, and goals, the producer will help the artist select the material to be recorded. The right song can play a crucial part in the success or failure of the artist's recordings. The producer will first look to any songs the artist might have written. If the artist doesn't write, or if his material is not appropriate, he'll survey music publishers and other writers for material that would suit his style.

After songs with sufficient commercial appeal have been selected, the artist and producer will work on an arrangement of the song that compliments the artist's style and enhances its commercial appeal. If needed, the producer will employ the services of a professional arranger, usually on a flat-fee basis.

Selecting the Studio and Essential Personnel

The next decision to be made is the selection of a recording studio, engineer, musicians, and background vocalists.

Today, fully equipped, professional-quality recording studios can be found throughout the country, not just in recording centers such as New York, Los Angeles, and Nashville. Million-selling records have been recorded in such small towns as Macon, Georgia and Muscle Shoals, Alabama, as well as in big cities like Chicago, Miami, and San Francisco. Because of this diversity of facilities, geographic location of a recording studio is not really an important consideration.

Most studios furnish a recording engineer as part of the

studio rental cost. This person's job is to attend to the technical end of recording, working under the supervision of the producer. Oftentimes, an established artist or producer may want to bring in his own engineer. In other instances, the producer may double as the engineer.

Experienced studio musicians can make a difference in the artist's recordings from both a quality and cost standpoint. A professional with studio experience works faster and with better results than a musician not accustomed to studio work. The same can be said of background vocalists.

Unlike the location of the studio, geography can play a significant role in the quality of musicians and vocalists. Experienced session men are found in recording centers because of the opportunity for steady work. Nashville and Los Angeles are both known for the quality of their studio musicians and vocalists. Other large centers such as New York, Detroit, Philadelphia, and Memphis, among others, are home to quality session men. Many studios have their own staff musicians who can provide solid basic rhythm tracks. Another approach is to employ the artist's band members on the session. Because of the uniformity of equipment, it's not uncommon for an artist to record his basic tracks in one city and later add horns, strings, and backup vocals in a studio located in a recording center.

Studio rental is usually handled on an hourly basis, depending on the number of tracks used and other specialized equipment available. Most master sessions employ 16- or 24-track professional recording equipment. The basic hourly rate will vary depending on equipment location and volume of recording activity. The rate for a top flight, multitrack studio can be as much as $150 per hour and up. The artist, manager, and producer should shop around for the best rate available. Studios often will block-book time at cheaper rates or offer a reduction for non-prime time periods.

Musicians who play on master sessions are paid in accordance with applicable American Federation of Musicians (A. F. of M.) scale rates. Vocalists' payments are gov-

erned by the American Federation of Television and Radio
Artists (AFTRA). These respective organizations should be
contacted by the manager as to applicable rates and procedures.

Rehearsals

An artist recording for the first time shouldn't tackle a full-
scale master session until he's gained recording experience. Most studios offer less-expensive demo rates on 4- or
8-track equipment. Band members or other less experienced musicians can be employed for this purpose. Union
rules provide for a reduction in scale payments on demo
sessions. The demo session is an excellent means to gain
experience while trying out different material and production techniques.

Once an artist feels that he has sufficient recording experience, commercial material, and satisfactory arrangements, he should try to rehearse this material with his musicians, if possible, or prepare written charts that they can
study. Because of cost considerations, the studio is no
place to rehearse.

Multi-track equipment employed in professional studios
allows each separate instrument and voice part to be recorded separately, making it possible to refine and perfect
a recording until it captures the exact sound desired by the
artist and his producer. After all parts of a song are recorded, the producer will mix the volume levels, tones, and
effects on the various tracks into the final master product.
Like anything else, experience and familiarity with the recording process contribute to better, more commercial recordings. The new artist should gain as much experience
as possible before he undertakes a full master session.

Securing a Recording Contract

Assuming producer, artist, and manager are satisifed they
have recorded a commercially viable master or a high-quality demo, the next step is to shop the tapes with record
companies in order to secure a recording contract. This
aspect of the manager's job is one of the most difficult, es-

pecially if he's dealing with a new or relatively unknown artist.

It's important for the manager or other persons charged with the responsibility of shopping tapes to know how to approach a record company and appreciate what they're looking for in a new artist. This knowledge, used wisely, will improve the artist's chances for success. To do this, the manager should try to put himself in the shoes of the record company.

What Does the Record Company Want?

Record companies are in business to do one thing—sell records. When a label signs a new artist, they're making a business decision that involves the commitment of substantial expenditures, not only in the form of royalty advances to cover recording costs, but also the costs of manufacturing, promotion, and tour support. One label executive estimates that every time he signs a new act, his company will spend a minimum of $100,000. He goes on to point out that this figure is usually low, and doesn't include any extra promotional efforts or the man-hours of his staff. Because of this expense, the company wants to be sure that they're dealing with an artist capable of recouping this amount and earning a profit for the company. Many factors go into this decision.

First and foremost, the record companies are looking for artists with talent and ability, capable of making records that will appeal to the mass record-buying public. Being good or just having talent isn't enough. Record company A & R men hear hundreds of good tapes by talented artists every year. They're looking for more. They want a unique voice or a distinct sound. Something that isn't already on the market. The worst thing a manager can say to a record company is, "I've got an artist who sounds just like. . . ." The companies aren't interested, because that aspect of the record market is covered.

When evaluating a record, the company is listening primarily for the lead voice. Except in exceptional cases, musicianship can be recreated by experienced session men;

however, the voice cannot. If the voice is unique, then the record must be commercial. The record company would soon go broke if their records didn't sell. Commerciality is a fluid concept that depends on many variables. The producer, artist, and manager must be aware of the marketplace when making an assessment of what is acceptable and what is not. This will vary, depending on the circumstances of each individual artist and the trends that exist at a given point in time in the entertainment industry.

The record company is also interested in the artist's material. Does he write his own songs? If not, what is the source of his material? The record company generally considers the ability of an artist to write his own songs as an asset, since it insures a constant source of material for future recordings. However, we're not suggesting that an artist must write his own material, although, in some cases, this could be a factor in the company's decision to sign an artist/writer when a non-writing artist of equal ability is available.

A critical aspect of the artist's career from the record company's point of view is the live personal appearance. Many labels won't sign an artist who's not a working act. Concert and club appearances are one of the most effective means of promotion a record company possesses. If the artist isn't able to perform his recorded material in a live performance situation, this promotional tool is lost. This illustrates the importance of obtaining live personal appearance experience before approaching a record company.

Aside from the artistic components of an artist's career, record companies want assurances that they'll be dealing with professionals with a realistic and cooperative attitude. If this element isn't present, many companies will choose not to sign an artist who may have met all the other criteria.

A critical area of inquiry is the artist's management. A good record company, just like a good manager, thinks in terms of careers, not just one-shot hit records. This is especially true because few first albums recoup the total investment the company has made in the artist. Often, it may take two, three, or even more album releases to break an artist. If an artist has ineffective management or no management at all, the company will often choose not to take a chance on him. In some cases, the record company will try to help the artist establish a management relationship. The major labels consider strong management to be a must for any artist.

As with management, the record company will want to inquire about the status of the artist's booking agency affiliation. This goes hand-in-hand with insuring that the artist has a tight, well-rehearsed concert and club act.

Other members of the artist's development team are also of interest to the label. They include his record producer, music publisher, publicity firm, and others.

The artist's attitude, maturity, and experience will weigh heavily on the company's ultimate decision. Talent isn't enough. The record company must be able to work with the artist on a very personal level. Unless the artist is realistic and willing to help build his own career, neither record company, management, nor anyone else will be able to make him a success. A company would rather pass up a promising artist than sign him and the potential headaches he may cause later.

The foregoing considerations have dealt with factors within the artist's control. However, there are other elements in the decision-making process that have nothing to do with the merits of the artist and his management.

A record company may be overcommitted to artists already on the label. In some cases, the company's budget may have been expended on signing new acts during the then-current fiscal year. There may be an overabundance of artists already signed who are similar in style and appeal to a particular new artist trying to get a deal. In some instances, a company may have recently gone through an internal shakeup resulting in a halt being ordered regarding acquisition of new artists.

A manager can improve his artist's chances for a deal by studying the artist rosters of various labels to determine the needs of the various companies. For instance, a label may be overloaded with female rock singers, but may need a male country artist.

The manager should read the trade magazines for news about company shakeups, shifts in emphasis, and expansion moves. So, often, knowing when to approach a label can mean the difference between a rejection and a record contract.

How Should the Company be Approached?

We've reviewed the general points a record company uses in its decision-making process. With these in mind, let's turn to how a company should be approached.

As stated in an earlier chapter, record companies aren't interested in dealing with amateurs or thrillseekers. They're in business to make money, not to educate people about the entertainment business. Record executives want to deal with professionals. To do this, they often rely on recommendations from others in the business they know and respect. The best way to get an appointment is by either knowing someone personally at the label or someone else in the business who can recommend the artist or help set up an appointment. Often an entertainment attorney or someone else associated with the artist such as the producer, will be more effective than the manager because of a personal contact.

If a manager has no personal contacts, he should get the name of someone in the A & R (Artist and Repertoire) Department and try to make an appointment. It is the A & R man's job to listen to tapes submitted to the record company. When communicating with the A & R man, the manager should be as professional as possible. This means being organized, brief, and to the point. Some A & R men will set up an appointment, others will ask the manager to mail them a copy of the tape. Of course, an appointment is more desirable. However, if the A & R man wants to listen to the tape in the privacy of his office, which many do, the manager should at least try to deliver the tape personally and establish some sort of rapport with him. The manager must be persistent, without making a pest of himself.

According to all the record-company executives we

surveyed, unsolicited mailing of tapes to record companies, almost without exception, is a waste of time. It's also generally a good idea for the artist to let either his manager or some other party make contact with the record company rather than do it himself.

When submitting an artist to a record company, the manager should generally make a tape copy of the two or three most commercial recordings the artist has done. In some cases, the manager may want to submit an entire album, depending on the preference of the company. An A & R man doesn't have time to sift through a number of recordings. If he's interested in the two or three best songs, he'll ask to hear more.

The manager should also submit a press kit that includes photographs of the artist, a professionally written biography, a list of past appearances, an itinerary of upcoming performances, and any other relevant information that will help the company better evaluate the artist.

During the interview, the manager should give the A & R man basic information about the artist in a straightforward manner. Record companies don't want hype. Neither do they want excuses made about the tape, such as, "You have to take into consideration that the mix isn't very good" or, "The artist had a cold when this tape was recorded." If the tape is a demo, the manager should give him that information. If it's a master, the manager can tell him so if he feels it would be helpful. If there's immediate interest in the tape, the manager might offer to take the A & R man to a live performance. The key to a successful interview is to be firm and remain in control, without becoming obnoxious.

Even if the A & R man shows interest, he'll almost always want to play the tape for others at the label. The manager should give the A & R man his card and tell him that he'll follow up the interview after he's had a chance to hear the tapes.

At the worst, the manager will get an on-the-spot rejection. In this case, he must stay cool. There's no sense in arguing; the A & R man's mind is made up. Instead, the manager should ask how to improve his artist's recordings the next time around. He should try to establish a rapport that might help get him in the door the next time. Then, regardless of the outcome of the interview, the manager should write a letter thanking the A & R man for his time and consideration of his artist.

In the event the tape is rejected, it's important that the manager and artist not become discouraged and give up. Rejection by record companies is just part of the business they must get used to. There are many stories of record companies rejecting artists and material that later went on to become hits. Even the Beatles were turned down by a number of companies before they were eventually signed to a recording contract. This fact should serve as inspiration to any artist and manager who have ever received a turn down. Just make the best of it, and move on.

Negotiating the Recording Contract

In the event the record company does become interested in the artist and wants to add him to their roster, artist and manager must turn their attention to negotiation of the recording contract.

The first step is to retain an experienced attorney specializing in entertainment law. He'll be able to advise the artist and manager of the complexities involved and points to be covered. Even if the manager has knowledge and experience in this area, it's still best in most cases to let the attorney do the negotiating. This course of action shields the artist and manager from the bargaining process, which can often be tedious and sometimes damaging to the artist/manager–record-company relationship.

Whichever approach is selected, both artist and manager should keep in mind that a record-company affiliation is a business relationship, regardless of how enthusiastic or friendly the A & R Department has been. The record-company negotiator, who is usually someone from the label's Business Affairs Department, will be trying to get the best terms possible for his company. From his point of view, signing a new artist is a dollars and cents proposition. The label takes advantage of its relative bargaining strength wherever possible. Naturally, the company will be in a better position when attempting to sign a new artist than it will be in negotiating a renewal of an established artist's contract or signing someone with a past track record.

With this basic premise in mind, we'll briefly discuss some of the points that should be considered by the manager in a record-contract negotiation. This is by no means meant to be a comprehensive or exhaustive discussion, but only a general outline of relevant considerations. This is far too complex a subject to deal with on an in-depth basis in the context of this book. The manager should seek the advice and counsel of his attorney in any record negotiation. Remember, that once the contract is signed, the artist and manager will likely have to live with its terms for a long time. This should give the artist and his representative more incentive to make sure that it's the best possible contract that can be negotiated under the circumstances.

Provisions of the Contract

Generally, the recording contract is an exclusive-personal-services agreement whereby the artist furnishes master recordings embodying his unique vocal and/or musical performances to the record company. In turn, it's their obligation to manufacture, promote, and market these records to the public, and pay the artist a royalty on the records sold. While this sounds simple enough in the abstract, the process is quite complicated and involved.

Royalties. One of the most important provisions of the contract, from the artist's point of view, is the artist's royalty. Royalties are usually based on either a percentage of the suggested retail price or the manufacturer's wholesale price. The royalty range can run from as low as 4% of retail up to as much as 12% or even more for superstar recording artists. These figures are usually doubled if royalties are computed on the wholesale price. Often, where a contract contains option periods, as most do, an escalating royalty rate is provided. It's also possible to negotiate rate increases or bonuses based upon sales performance. Advances recoupable against royalties is another subject area for negotiation.

A crucial factor in royalty computations involves various deductions and rate reductions for specific types of sales. An experienced attorney will try to minimize these as much as possible, depending upon the artist's bargaining position.

Industry custom provides that royalties be computed on 90% of records sold. This 10% deduction was originally devised to cover breakage. Although breakage is not the problem it once was due to improved manufacturing techniques, the custom remains, though in some cases it can be either reduced or eliminated.

There's also a customary deduction for jacketing or packaging costs. This figure usually runs from 10% to 15% for records and from 15% to 25% for tapes, which usually retail at about $1.00 more than records. The packaging costs should be limited as much as possible and specified in the contract. It's also standard to deduct all applicable excise taxes and duties applicable to the records.

Finally, the artist and manager should be aware that it's standard in the record industry to pay royalties only on records sold, and not on those returned by the distributors. There's generally a 100% return privilege accorded to distributors on any unsold product. As a result, most record companies will withhold a percentage of an artist's royalties computed on records shipped, in order to cover returns. The attorney should try to limit this figure as much as possible and provide for prompt liquidation of the reserve after a stated number of accounting periods.

Besides deductions from amounts payable, there are also various reductions in the applicable percentage payable in certain specialized sales areas. For example, a lesser royalty rate of 50% of the normal retail sales percentage is applied to record-club sales, budget records, tape sales, educational sales, records sold to military bases, and foreign sales. Generally, no royalty is paid on disc jockey or promotional copies or bonus of free goods given away by record clubs to generate new membership. The artist's attorney should strive to minimize these reductions whenever possible, as well as limit the discretion of the company in areas of budget records and free goods.

Finally, the artist and manager should be aware that in most cases, all recording costs paid by the company are deemed to be advances against future royalties that will be recouped before any payment is made to the artist. Efforts should be made to specifically define these costs and if possible, avoid cross-collateralization of recoupment of one record against royalties earned by other records. The record company will generally resist this approach, especially with a new artist.

For those artists and managers who feel the record company is taking an unfair advantage of the artist through low royalty rates and various deductions and rate reductions, it should be pointed out that few first albums by new artists recoup the company's investment. It takes a substantial financial and personal commitment on the part of the record company to break an artist. The label is trying to protect itself as much as possible. Without many of these devices, a record company could simply not afford to sign as many new artists as they do. It should also be noted that an artist can dramatically improve his bargaining position through sales performance, thus becoming more valuable to the label. This will help him gain more concessions and higher royalties in the future.

Length of the Contract. Another area of importance to the artist is the length or term of the contract. Standard procedure is to make the term one year with a number of additional one-year options usually exercisable at the election of the record company. Depending on the particular state in which the contract is entered, there may be restrictions on the maximum number of option periods. For example, California limits any contract involving personal services to seven years. More stringent restrictions are involved when the artist is a minor. An approach often used is to make the contract for a term of one year, with four successive one-year option periods.

From the artist's standpoint, the attorney should seek to limit the number of option periods as much as possible, unless there are substantial guarantees involved. If the artist is successful, a shorter term will allow him to renegotiate sooner. If he's unsuccessful or becomes unhappy, a shorter term allows him the freedom to seek an alternate record affiliation.

Recording and Release Requirements. Recording and release requirements are another vital area of artist concern. The contract will set forth a minimum number of record sides or compositions which must be recorded by the artist and delivered to the company in each year of the agreement. Generally, the company will advance the costs of the recordings and will usually have the option to require that more sides be recorded. Normally, the company is under no obligation to release any of the artist's recordings. The artist's negotiations should seek some type of release commitment from the company. Usually the requirement to release a specified number of records during any one year of the contract is a precondition to the exercise of the next option period by the company.

Promotional Support. Another important element in contract negotiations, especially for the new artist, is promotional support. The artist will seek financial commitment from the record company in the form of trade ads, media time buys, and other forms of advertising.

Tour Support. Another form of involvement is tour support. The artist will request that the label help finance his personal appearances to enable him to promote his records. Tour support is usually in the form of direct cash subsidy or label responsibility for any expense deficit incurred by the artist in connection with a particular tour. The strength and ability of the manager and booking agent and the types and importance of dates the artist will play will weigh heavily on the company's decision in this area. The company doesn't want to commit money to help promote a tour that will be mismanaged or ineffective.

Artistic Control. Artistic control of the material to be recorded is a point often considered vital to an artist. This right is often granted to established artists with a sales track record. It's not granted as often to a new artist because of inexperience and lack of sales history. As a practical matter, the A & R Department and artist/manager/producer will work together in the selection of material, with the company reserving veto power in the event of a dispute.

Royalty Accounting. Royalty accounting procedures are extremely important to the artist. Most companies account semiannually. The artist should always seek the right to audit the company's books of account at reasonable intervals. A procedure should be set up to enable the artist to terminate the agreement in the event of nonpayment of royalties or other material breaches by the company. Companies will often oppose this type of clause or seek to word it very narrowly.

These are just some of the major elements of the recording contract from the artist's standpoint. We again stress the importance of an attorney in the negotiation process.

Summary
As mentioned earlier, the record contract is strictly a business relationship. The company will, whenever possible, try to negotiate terms favorable to itself. By the same token, the artist and manager should try to gain as many concessions and compromises as possible. Often, the record company will be accommodating on certain points and inflexible on others. The key point to remember is that the label's negotiator won't offer concessions; the artist's representative will have to ask.

14.
Music Publishing

One of the most complex, least understood, yet most important aspects of the entertainment industry is music publishing. An in-depth treatment of this intricate subject, however, is beyond the scope of this book. Our purpose here is to deal with music publishing only as it relates to artist management.

Confusion over the subject is not confined just to the beginner. Many experienced artist managers confess to knowing very little when it comes to the subject of music publishing. This isn't surprising. Publishing requires among other things, a working knowledge of domestic and foreign copyright laws, experience in negotiating and administering detailed contracts, an understanding of how performing rights societies and mechanical collection agencies are structured, and in-depth experience in royalty accounting, not to mention the ability to recognize and help develop a good song. No wonder so many people are in the dark.

Before discussing the interplay of management and publishing, it's first necessary to grasp the basic function of the music publisher and the structure of this aspect of the entertainment business.

The Music Publisher

The music publisher's world revolves around the song. In fact, the publisher will invariably tell you that the song is the foundation of the music industry. Without it, there'd be no artists, no managers, no record companies, and no booking agents. Undoubtedly, there's a great deal of truth in this statement. The song is indeed a necessary component to the success of any recording artist or concert performer.

Conceding the importance of the song, the more specific question is, "What exactly does a publisher do with the song?" Briefly stated, the function of a music publisher is to locate and commercially develop songs (often referred to as "copyrights") in much the same way that a manager locates and develops artists' careers. In both cases, publisher and manager are working to transform artistic potential into a realization of success.

The music publisher searches for songs and songwriters with ability and potential. When the publisher finds a song that he feels has commercial potential, he acquires the publishing rights in return for a promise to pay the writer a royalty based on gross income earned from the commercial exploitation of the composition. He'll protect the song by obtaining a copyright registration on the words and music. An active publisher will work with the writer to perfect the song or possibly help develop and improve his writing style. Tape demos and lead sheets will be made. Once the song is in final form, the music publisher will try to match it with a recording artist to whose style he feels the song would fit, hoping the artist will record it or use it in his television or personal live appearances. The reason a publisher will expend the time and money to accomplish these tasks is simple. Every time an artist sells a record embodying the song, the music publisher and songwriter make money. Every time the song is performed on television or radio, the publisher and writer make money. Every time a copy of sheet music or a printed folio containing the song is sold, the publisher and writer make money. Every time the song is used in motion picture soundtrack, the publisher and writer make money. When income is realized, it's the job of the publisher to collect the money and account to the writer for his share of the proceeds. He retains the balance representing the publisher's share.

The foregoing is an oversimplified account of the publisher's role. The process involves endless hours of listening to tapes, changing lyrics, reassuring songwriters, and all of the other things that go into finding and perfecting a hit song. This is followed by seemingly unending streams of contracts, memos, letters, forms, phone calls, and tape copies.

Success for the music publisher is measured by how many times a particular song is recorded, how many times it's played on radio and TV, and how many records are sold. The more recordings, performances, and record sales, the more money is earned for the songwriter and his publisher.

From a management standpoint, the music publisher should first of all be viewed as a source of material for his artist. Many recording artists don't write their own material and therefore must depend totally on songs written by others. Many other artists who do write are not consistently able to turn out quality songs suited to their own recording styles. These artists find it necessary to supplement their own songs with material of others. Even the great singer/songwriters such as Neil Diamond or Paul Simon will on occasion record songs written by others if they feel the material is hit caliber. Every artist needs good material to sustain his career. As a result, most artists will be open to the possibility of recording someone else's song.

A manager, artist, or producer seeking material should realize that a music publisher is only too happy to submit songs for consideration by the artist. While this is especially true of an established artist with a recording contract, it also applies to a new artist trying to secure his first deal. For this reason, the manager or artist should not shy away from the major publishing houses when seeking material. Nor should the manager overlook the smaller companies also trying to establish themselves. Often, a lesser known company will expend more effort than a larger firm to find the right song for a new artist, hoping to build a relationship with him and his manager.

When approaching a music publisher for songs, the manager, producer, or artist should speak with the professional manager or someone in the Professional Department. This department is very similar to the A & R Department of a record company. It's the Professional Department's job to find, develop, and polish new songs and match them with artists. The professional man is also involved in adapting previously recorded songs to the styles of currently popular artists.

When approaching the professional manager, the artist or manager should specify the type of material that the artist records or performs, such as country, soft rock, ballads, and the like. The professional manager should also be given a tape of two or three songs indicative of the artist's singing style and voice quality. This helps the Professional Department identify songs that might be appropriate for the artist. If the artist has a certain tempo, instrumentation, or sound in mind, let the publisher know this also. It's also helpful for the manager, producer, or artist to specify whether he's looking for previously unrecorded material or proven copyrights which could be given a new arrangement. The distinction can be important from a legal standpoint.

The United States Copyright Act, which went into effect January 1, 1978, gives the copyright owner (usually the publisher) the right to determine the first artist to commercially record a particular song. But after the song has been recorded and distributed to the public for the first time, anyone has the right to re-record it without permission from the copyright owner, provided that they pay the owner a royalty set by the Copyright Act. This part of the Copyright Act is commonly referred to as the "Compulsory Licensing" provision. Because of this legal requirement, the artist can't record a previously unrecorded work without the copyright owner's permission. The manager, producer, or record company should therefore make sure that permission to record the work is granted by the copyright owner before the song is actually recorded.

Another consideration in recording new or unproven material controlled by a music publisher is to insure that the song hasn't been recorded earlier by another artist who might release the record ahead or at the same time of the artist's release, thereby creating a competitive relationship between records. While a publisher can't always guarantee a first recording, especially in the case of previously recorded but unproven material, he can let the manager know of other artists to whom the song has been submitted.

If the artist is of sufficient stature or is seriously interested in recording a new copyright, the manager or producer might request the publisher grant an "exclusive" on the song. This means that the publisher won't show the song to anyone else for a stated period of time to enable the artist and record company sufficient time to record and release the song.

Another aspect of recording previously unrecorded material is the possibility of a participation by the artist in the publishing income from the song as an inducement for the artist to record it. This is a practice that is obviously unpopular with music publishers. However, an established recording artist with a large record-buying following can, in some instances, persuade a publisher to give up either part ownership of the copyright (publisher's share only) or a percentage of the income earned from the sale of the particular record version by the artist by the lure of automatic sales and performances. Many publishers have policies against such practices, arguing that the integrity of their copyrights should remain intact. Other publishers maintain that there's never any guarantee a particular recording will be a hit, thus there's no justification in giving up part-ownership or potential income.

Besides providing an artist with quality material, many publishers contribute to the promotion of a record embodying their copyrights. At this point, the music publisher becomes a member of the artist's development team. Often, a manager can persuade the publisher to either purchase or co-op a trade advertisement or employ independent radio promotion men. Some of the larger publishing companies have their own promotion staffs to compliment the efforts of the record company. An active publisher is also an excellent source of information as to the radio airplay and sales activity of a particular record.

The manager is well-advised to develop contacts with quality music publishers to insure a steady flow of material for his artist. An experienced publisher will always be thinking of material for the artist and won't waste a manager's time by submitting weak or inappropriate material.

In the event the artist does record a song controlled by an active music publisher, especially in the case of an "A side" single release, the manager should keep the company informed of all pertinent developments. This will help insure a maximum contribution by the publisher to the success of the artist's record.

Music Publishing as Income

Let's now examine music publishing as a source of income for the artist/writer. The ability of the artist not only to perform but also to write his own songs adds an important dimension to his career. First of all, a singer/songwriter is guaranteed a steady source of material geared to his vocal and musical style. This guarantee of material generally makes the artist more attractive to record companies, booking agents, and managers than an artist who must depend on the writing of others. Secondly, the artist/writer has a much greater income potential than the nonwriter. For example, the Beatles were an extremely successful group, with all four artists sharing equally in record royalties and personal appearances. However, John Lennon and Paul McCartney, who wrote the majority of the group's original songs, far surpassed the other members in earning power as a result of their songwriting royalties.

The problem confronting the manager of an artist/writer is how to maximize the long-term and short-term income derived from the artist's works. The answer to this question depends on the particular circumstances of the artist and on the alternatives available to him.

Before considering the artist's publishing alternatives, let's briefly review the nature and sources of income that can be derived from the exploitation of copyrighted musical compositions. Generally, a writer will, by contract, convey all rights of ownership in and to the musical composition to the publisher. This grant includes the right to secure copyright protection in the name of the publisher. In return, the publisher agrees to use his best efforts to commercially develop and exploit the song and to pay the writer a percentage of the proceeds. We refer to this royalty as the writer's share and the balance as the publisher's share.

Income is realized from five main sources: mechanical royalties derived from the sale of records and tapes embodying the song; radio and television performances; movie synchronization fees; sale of printed music; and miscellaneous usages. Most standard songwriter contracts call for mechanical, performance, synchronization, and miscellaneous income to be divided 50% to the writer and the remaining 50% to the publisher. A lesser percentage or set amount is paid to the writer as a royalty on the sale of printed music. This reduced payment takes into consideration the publisher's expense in printing, distributing, and selling sheet music and folios.

Royalties from the Sale of Records and Tapes. The Copyright Act of 1978 sets a statutory rate of compensation that must be paid to copyright owners by anyone who manufactures and distributes records embodying the owner's composition in lieu of a negotiated rate. The statutory rate is 2 3/4¢ or 1/2¢ per minute or fraction thereof, whichever is larger for each record manufactured and distributed. Assuming an artist/writer writes ten compositions embodied on an album that sells 100,000 units at the statutory mechanical royalty rate, the total amount of mechanical royalties payable to the copyright owner would be $27,500 assuming there are no deductions for collection fees. Of this sum, $13,750 would represent the writer's share and the remaining $13,750 would be retained by the publisher. Although payment is computed in pennies, they can mount up in a hurry if a hit record is involved.

Performing Rights. A second lucrative source of income consists of performing rights. The performing rights of publishers and writers in the United States are controlled by three performing-rights societies, ASCAP, BMI and SESAC. ASCAP and BMI control the bulk of all compositions written in this country. SESAC is a much smaller, privately owned society specializing in certain areas of music. The societies license radio and television broadcasters as well as concert halls, nightclubs, and other users of music. Each respective society has a complicated payment system whereby it distributes the proceeds from these licenses to its publisher and writer members based on the number and type of performances of the respective copyrighted musical compositions they represent.

Movie Synchronization Fees. Movie synchronization fees account for another source of musical copyright income. Songs are usually licensed for use by the publisher on a negotiated fee basis. Producers of major motion pictures are willing to pay substantial amounts for a license to use the "right" song in their productions.

Sale of Printed Music. Printed music consists of individual sheet music and song folios containing multiple compositions. This has proven to be an expanding source of revenue especially with the popularity of the "personality folio" which features songs in printed form that have been made popular by the recordings of a particular artist.

Miscellaneous Uses. Miscellaneous uses of material include use of songs on greeting cards and song quotes used in books and articles.

It's clear from this overview of potential income sources how much a successful artist/writer stands to gain from a hit song. The question facing the manager is how to realize maximum benefits while still allowing time for other career pursuits such as recording, touring, commercials, television, and personal appearances.

Finding a Publisher

The most obvious course of action is to find an experienced music publisher to handle an artist's songs. This is especially advisable in the case of a new unproven writer without a recording contract that will insure him an outlet for his material. An active, experienced music publisher who believes in a writer can offer him a variety of services otherwise unavailable to him. One of the most attractive features of this type of arrangement is that a reputable publisher's fee is based entirely on a percentage of earnings from the writer's songs.

By choosing this option, the artist/writer and manager take advantage of the publisher's expertise in copyright law, publishing, administration, song development, promotion, and exploitation. They also save the cost of obtaining copyright protection, preparation of lead sheets, production of demos, and costs associated with submitting the songs to other recording artists. The major drawback is that the writer gives up approximately 50% of potential earnings in the form of the publisher's share.

The artist/writer has two alternate ways of working with a publisher to exploit his songs, depending on the strength of his writing and the desires of the parties. He can either publish on a song-by-song basis, or he can elect to sign an exclusive writer agreement whereby all songs written during the term of the agreement will be submitted to the publisher. If the latter approach is chosen, the writer should usually expect to receive a sum of money as a signing bonus or cash advance recoupable against future writer royalties.

When selecting a music publisher, it's important that the artist and manager choose a legitimate, active publisher who will work to secure recordings of the writer's songs rather than merely act as a "copyright collector." This type of publisher finds songs, signs songwriter contracts, and then deposits them in a filing cabinet hoping something will happen either through the efforts of the writer or perhaps with luck.

The writer should feel comfortable with his publisher and be able to relate to the company's personnel on a personal level. This is important if the publisher really intends to help the writer develop his songwriting skills and techniques.

Even though artist/writers may be convinced of a publisher's sincerity, it's also important that the publisher has the time to devote to exploiting the writer's songs. There's nothing worse than for a writer to be lost in the shuffle, especially when he's writing commercial material.

Regardless of whether the artist/writer chooses to work with a publisher on a per song or exclusive basis, he should seek the help of an attorney experienced in music publishing to negotiate and draft his contract. While many contractual terms are more or less standard, many others are not.

Important items to be considered include the scope of rights granted, duration of the contract, territory, royalty rates, deductions from writer's royalties, time and method of royalty payments, right to audit publisher's books, and royalty advances or guarantees. Foreign aspects of the publisher's contract will be dealt with in a later chapter.

The main trap a writer wants to avoid is granting publishing rights to a publisher who's either unwilling or unable to exploit his songs. Depending on the bargaining strength of the parties and the importance of the writer and song, the artist/writer's negotiator may request that a clause be inserted in the contract whereby all rights to a particular song will revert to the writer after a stated period of time if the publisher hasn't been successful in securing a commercial recording of the song. Many publishers object to this type of clause, maintaining it may take an investment of considerable money and time to commercially exploit a writer's songs. Such a recapture clause would undermine the total commitment necessary to achieve this success. This argument is particularly valid if the publisher has advanced unrecouped monies to the writer. But certain companies won't object, provided that they're given a reasonable time to secure a recording and the writer agrees to re-pay any unrecouped advances against royalties.

The Artist as Publisher

An alternative available to the artist/writer who doesn't want to work with an established publisher is to act as his own publisher or let his manager or another employee ad-minister his catalog. This is most often done by an estab-lished recording artist who writes all or substantially all of his own material. This type of undertaking requires suffi-cient financial resources to hire persons with publishing ex-perience or a manager with sufficient time and experience to handle this additional responsibility.

The advantage of this arrangement is obvious. The artist retains not only the writer's share but the publisher's share of the income as well. But the disadvantages are many. First, the artist/writer must bear all the expenses that would otherwise be borne by the publisher. Because of the lack of an organized staff, the artist/publisher may not be as effec-tive in obtaining recordings of his material by other artists as a regular publisher. Finally, unless the artist or someone on his staff has experience in the field of publishing admin-istration, the artist could jeopardize his entire catalog.

There are also other drawbacks. Normally, publishing administration doesn't come within the normal scope of management duties. Many managers simply aren't quali-fied to undertake this very complex and multi-faceted job. Even if a manager is qualified, he may not have sufficient time to devote to the management of the artist's career as well as administration of his publishing affairs. But if the manager does decide to undertake these duties, a separ-ate agreement covering the scope of his publishing duties and compensation is advisable. In this event, the manager and artist may want to modify the management agreement to exempt publishing income realized by the artist's publishing firm from the income base on which the man-ager's fee or percentage is computed, provided, of course, that the manager is receiving separate compensation for his publishing activities.

The structure and operation of the artist's publishing company is beyond the scope of this book. However, the artist and manager are advised to consult an attorney thoroughly knowledgeable in the area of music publishing. He can provide counsel on the advisability of such a move and can help organize and structure the artist's publishing operations. The respective performing rights organizations and mechanical collection agencies should also be consulted regarding their rules and procedures.

Other Alternatives

For many artist/writers, especially those with record company affiliations and established followings, there may be alternatives that a manager might consider that fall between writing for an established publisher and acting as a self-contained publisher.

The first of these arrangements is a joint ownership agreement with an established publisher. Often, a name recording artist/writer with a guaranteed outlet for his recorded product has sufficient leverage to enter into an agreement whereby a music publishing company owned by him and a full-time, active publisher can jointly own the copyrights to his songs. This allows the artist to take advantage of the active publisher's administrative, exploitative, and promotional capabilities while still collecting his writer's share and a portion of the publisher's share of income. Although the artist gives up part of his copyright ownership, he's still able to increase his income and maximize the long-term development of his copyrights.

Another approach is an agency representation agreement with an active publisher. This is similar to joint ownership, except full copyright ownership remains vested in the artist/writer's company. The established publisher is paid a percentage of the total publisher's share of income but only from monies earned or accruing during the term of the agency agreement. Obviously, the inducement to a major publisher to enter into this type of arrangement is not nearly as attractive as a full or joint copyright ownership arrangement.

A third alternative is an administration or collection agreement with a major publisher or a publishing administration service company. Here the artist's publishing company retains an administrative specialist to render specific services such as copyright registration, performing right clearance, and administration and/or royalty collection and accounting in return for a negotiated fee or percentage of publishing income.

One last alternative that must be considered is the possibility of the artist publishing his material through a company owned or controlled by the artist's manager or jointly owned by artist and manager. This raises possible conflict-of-interest problems with the manager. Will a manager in this situation be tempted to make a publishing decision that might be good for him personally but detrimental to his client's career? What happens to ownership of copyrights in the event of a breakup between the artist and manager? Finally, should the manager's fee be calculated on a percentage of the writer's share of income derived from material published by the manager's company? These are all potential problem areas. This isn't to say that such an arrangement isn't advisable. There's nothing wrong with it as long as there's full disclosure by the manager and artist of their positions, understood and agreed to by all respective parties. The best advice here is for the artist and manager to consult their attorneys as to the structure of any such arrangement.

Responsibilities of the Artist/Writer and Manager

Regardless of the publishing alternatives selected, both artist and manager should be aware that there are certain responsibilities related to songwriting and music publishing that are the sole responsibility of the writer and his representative.

The most notable of these is selection and affiliation with a performing rights society. Performance royalties are paid directly by the societies to publisher and writer members on a separate basis. A writer can only be affiliated with one society and must make that decision himself based on which society is best for him. As mentioned before, ASCAP and BMI are the leading societies in terms of license fees collected and royalties paid. SESAC has a smaller, more specialized membership. Performing rights societies are highly competitive and each offers certain advantages over the others. Their Membership Departments will be glad to talk to writers and managers concerning the relative merits of their respective organizations. The artist/writer and manager should be cautioned that failure to affiliate may result in loss of writer performance credits even though a song is copyrighted and published.

Once the writer has affiliated with the performing rights society, the writer member and his manager must deal with the society directly in the area of writer-related affairs. Although the publisher may offer guidance in this area, it's not his responsibility. The manager is well-advised to contact a representative of his client's society as to the duties and responsibilities of the writer.

There is no one "right" answer as to which music publishing alternative or performing rights society an artist and manager should select. The decision should hinge on what's right for the artist at a given stage of his career. Publishing and songwriting royalties are important long-term sources of income that can continue to accrue long after record royalties and personal appearance income have diminished or come to an end. As with career planning, careful development of copyrights should be the goal of every artist/songwriter. As a result, decisions in this area should not be made hastily. As in every other career area, the manager and artist should strive to educate themselves as to the mechanics and structure of publishing to enable selection of the best alternatives available. Awareness and knowledge of music publishing by a manager, accompanied by careful planning and intelligent decision-making, can result in long-term financial security for the artist and his manager.

15.
Television, Radio, and Motion Pictures

It's virtually impossible to be engaged in the entertainment industy and not be affected by the impact of commercial television. Network TV has significantly changed the character of entertainment around the world. Prior to television, an artist could reach a mass audience primarily through live network radio, which had only a fraction of the programming alternatives available through television or personal appearances. Television has changed all of this.

Television
Today, an appearance by an artist on the right television show can be seen by tens of millions. An artist's name can be turned into a household word literally in a matter of weeks. There's almost limitless potential for instant career acceleration.

The prospects for career development offered by television must, however, balance against the ever-present dangers inherent in the medium. The same mass exposure that can make an artist an instant success can just as quickly make him an overnight has-been. The artist and manager should temper their enthusiasm by being wary of the potential negative consequences of television.

Our purpose is to treat television as another career-building tool available to the musical artist, variety artist, dancer, or comedian, and his management. The chapter is not intended to be a detailed examination of the overall structure of the television industry. It's rather an overview of the situations an artist and manager will face in maximizing the effective use of this medium.

The artist's objectives and approach to TV will differ, depending on his particular situation. For instance, if the artist is an established singer/songwriter signed to a major record label, he'll most likely be interested in promoting his record sales, creating demand for his concert appearances, and generating interest in his songs, as well as maximizing his financial gain from television appearances. A relatively unknown standup comic without a record deal will have different motivations. He'll most likely be seeking future television appearances and club bookings while possibly hoping to use his TV exposure as a means to induce the interest of record companies.

Regardless of specifics, it's essential that the career plan contain specific television goals and guidelines to help the artist and manager intelligently select TV appearances that will contribute to the overall success of the plan. There's nothing more potentially damaging to a career than indiscriminate, randomly selected television appearances. The manager who adopts this policy or nonpolicy is flirting with disaster in the form of overexposure or negative image projection.

Types of Television Appearances. In order to formulate an effective television policy, let's first look at the television alternatives available to the established artist and the considerations that should go into his decisions regarding TV appearances.

Television producers, programmers, and sponsors are always looking for artists or celebrities with "name value" to enhance their programs. When evaluating name value or drawing power, they're generally looking for someone with wide national appeal rather than with a regional or a localized following. An artist's value is directly proportional to his current activities. A hit record, recent award, or national concert tour will undoubtedly make the artist more attractive. Visual appeal and personality are also factors considered by television professionals. Overall long-term career success is yet another consideration.

Depending on the degree of drawing power of an artist, he can generally look to the following television alternatives: host or guest on a TV Special; host or guest on a musical variety series or musical concept series; guest on a talk or game show; appearance on a segment of a dramatic series, mini-series, or made-for-TV movie. The most common types of appearances for the musical variety artist are Specials, talk shows, and musical variety or concept shows.

There are several avenues to television exposure for the established artist. The major multifaceted booking agencies maintain very strong contacts with the producers and talent coordinators of the network talk shows and musical variety and concept shows. A strong agency contact is often instrumental in getting an artist the "right" slot on the "right" show. Many of the major record companies also maintain contacts in this area because of the impact such appearances can have on promoting record sales. Many top-level managers also make it their business to maintain strong television contacts.

The talk show and musical variety or concept guest appearance should be viewed primarily as a promotional tool. Talk shows rarely pay guests above scale. From a career development standpoint, this should be the least of an artist's worries. Such an appearance can often be the one break the artist needs to boost him into the national limelight.

Financial remuneration for a musical variety or musical concept appearance can be more substantial, depending on the artist's name value and the budget of the particular show. However, just as with talk shows, money should not be the only factor considered. A slot on the right show can be of untold value to an artist in terms of promotion and exposure. A case in point is the first United States national television appearances of the Beatles on the Ed Sullivan Show in the early 1960s. This was the major push that helped launch the group in the United States. This exposure helped enable them to achieve superstar status in relatively short order.

The TV Special is probably the most attractive alternative available to the established artist from a financial, promotional, and artistic standpoint. This is especially true if he's able to exercise a measure of creative control over the program and guest selection process, which many do.

Here, the procedure is somewhat different than in the previous examples. Often the artist/manager and/or an independent television producer will formulate a concept for a Special and then sell it either to a television network or directly to a sponsor. Naturally, the more name value and following the artist possesses, the easier it will be to sell a Special.

In addition to hosting a Special, many established artists are often asked to appear on such programs as guests, many times at the invitation of the artist/host. Many major artists limit their television appearances only to this type of format to avoid problems of overexposure and negative image projection mentioned earlier.

Making the Selection. Regardless of the alternatives available to the artist, careful attention should be given to any television offer based on some of the following factors. First, the manager and artist should consider the type of show. Is its format consistent with the artist's image, career plan, and goals? For instance, a serious singer/songwriter would stand to gain little by a guest appearance on a TV quiz show or situation comedy. However, such a format might be consistent with a comedian's image and career objectives. The second factor to consider is the show's ratings. This will determine the exposure value of the particular program for the artist and may indicate the quality of the program and how it's perceived by the public. Then there is another consideration: Who are the other guest stars? The artist wants to be presented in the best possible light. The stature of other performers, billing, time slots, and so forth, will have a bearing on whether the artist will want to appear on the show.

Overexposure potential is also a major consideration. Too many TV appearances, regardless of their quality, can cause the public's interest in the artist to decline. Once the artist is too accessible on television, the concertgoer and record buyer won't be nearly as interested in paying to hear or see the artist when they can get the same thing free on television. There's also the danger that too many appearances will cause the audience to tire of the performer. Their adulation can quickly turn to indifference. This has ended the career of more than one artist. Making the right decision here isn't easy. It requires a great deal of judgment and perception on the part of the manager and the willingness to say "no" to lucrative offers for the sake of preserving the artist's career.

While we've spoken in terms of the established artist, the same guidelines are generally applicable to the new artist. The major difference is that the artist without established name value will find it much more difficult to get television exposure, especially the right exposure. The new artist should be encouraged to develop strong management, booking agency and record-company connections to help break the national TV exposure barrier. Other alternatives are regionally syndicated shows and local television as a means of gaining experience and exposure.

Radio

Aside from television, another important aspect of an artist's career, especially a recording artist, is radio. In the early 1950s, television succeeded in replacing radio as the primary vehicle for reaching the mass audience with the live performance. Almost simultaneous with this change came the increased importance of the phonograph record. As the radio networks dropped their variety-oriented entertainment and stations became more independent, there was a need for new programming ideas and concepts.

Likewise, the record companies needed new promotional avenues to help boost sales. The result was a shift to programming of records on radio stations that in the past had depended on network feeds of variety and comedy programs. This concept has grown since that time to the point today where AM and FM radio airplay is probably the most important promotional vehicle available to the record companies. This concept has also established itself as the lifeblood of radio programming.

It's essential that recording artists and managers realize and understand the crucial importance of radio airplay to their careers. Without it, the mass record-buying public will generally be unaware of not only the artist's records but most likely the artist himself. The strategic role radio plays is demonstrated by the significant sums of money record companies budget in order to promote radio airplay of their product. An awareness of the Promotion Department's job and the radio station's needs and objectives by the artist and manager will contribute greatly to the overall success of the artist and his records.

The primary rule every artist and record company should keep in mind regarding radio airplay is that radio stations are in business to make a profit. They can only make a profit if they can attract advertisers. Since advertisers are attracted by a station's ratings, the station's record playlist is formulated to obtain the best possible ratings. In other words, programming is not designed to help a record company or an artist sell records, though many artists and managers are unwilling to accept this reality.

Because ratings are all important, a top-forty AM station will program only those records it thinks will draw listeners. Playlists are usually restricted to between twenty and forty records. The records programmed are usually either already hits or have been recorded by hit artists with past track records. Very few new artists are added to these tight playlists. Those that are must have a record with super commercial appeal that's not too long, not too short, and fits into the station's format. It's a reality of the business.

While progressive FM, rhythm and blues, and country music stations may be a little less restrictive in their programming, the same general rules apply.

The artist and manager are urged to become familiar with primary and secondary radio stations in various markets around the country that have formats consistent with their recordings. Getting to know program directors and disc jockeys can often be helpful. Besides the radio people, the manager should also get to know the record company's promotion staff. Unless the promotion man believes in an artist's record, there's little chance he can convince a program director to program it.

Learning "radio" is a major educational project in itself, but well worth the effort. The importance of this aspect of entertainment to a recording artist and his manager cannot be overemphasized. It's important that the artist and manager understand and appreciate radio and radio promotion in order to effectively help themselves to reach their own career goals.

Motion Pictures

The final subject area dealt with in this chapter is motion pictures. This is a complex component of the entertainment industry, with its own peculiar language, regulations, rules, and complexities.

As with television, we want to deal with motion pictures from the standpoint of the musical/variety artist and his management. The motion picture industry offers the opportunity for long-term career maintenance to those artists who have the talent and ability to act. Just because a person is a successful recording artist doesn't necessarily mean that he'll be a successful actor. Although there have been successful recording artists and songwriters in the past who have possessed acting ability and screen appeal and have added this dimension of the entertainment industry to their careers, many others have not.

A manager is well advised to think in terms of possible involvement of his client in motion pictures as a career alternative or supplement that can be very rewarding both artistically and financially, provided his client genuinely has potential in this area. Attempting an acting career can detract from an artist's other endeavors if his efforts are not at least within the realm of an acceptable performance. The artist should be aware of what a bad movie can do to the recording or performing aspects of his career. For those artists making the transition, the manager will find that name value helps to get you in the door to see producers and studio executives. However, as with recording and personal appearances, it's the public that makes the final determination of the artist's acting abilities. The manager should be cautioned to seek the help of experienced motion picture professionals before attempting such a move.

16.
Personal
Appearances

One of the most lucrative aspects of the entertainment business for the artist is the personal appearance. A popular concert attraction can command substantial sums of money for a live performance. If the artist has a record high on the charts, coupled with an explosive stage show, the income derived from live performances can be staggering. Everyone associated with the artist benefits if he has the ability to make successful personal appearances. This ability to entertain live audiences can be used as a negotiating weapon by the manager when dealing with record companies, booking agents, and producers.

The artist capable of "turning on" an audience is helping the record company sell its product. A successful appearance either reinforces the artist's appeal to old fans or creates new followers. Every time the artist makes a successful personal appearance, his audience becomes a potential market for his records.

A dynamic live performance also translates into increased demand for the artist's services, consequently strengthening his position with booking agents. The artist who has promoters and other talent-buyers calling booking agents for him will naturally be in a much better negotiating position to increase his price or receive favorable percentage guarantees from buyers. The artist's live performance has the potential to outlive and outearn his recording career. Many artists who have been moderately successful in recording have maintained lucrative careers with strong live appearances. In many ways, the personal appearance is the lifeblood of an artist's career.

There are many different levels of live performances available to the artist. Depending on the success of an artist in the record market, and his style and type of performance, the manager can select the most favorable type of personal appearance for his artist-client. Basically, the alternatives available to the manager fall into three categories (excluding television and motion pictures, which previously have been discussed): clubs, private parties, and concerts. These broad categories can be divided into many levels, or what we refer to as "stages."

Clubs

The club portion of the live performance market can be divided into lounges, rock and show clubs, showcase clubs or listening rooms, and large hotels and national chains. The private party segment includes high school and fraternity parties, corporate parties, conventions, and other miscellaneous private functions. The concert level can be divided into the college market and promotions. .

Artists, ranging from the youngest to the most experienced professional, can find a market for their talent on one of these stages. The manager should select the most desirable stage from the standpoint of career development and artistic growth as well as income realization. As with other phases of the entertainment business, it's essential that the manager understand each area of the personal appearance.

Lounge. For the sake of our discussion, let's define a "lounge" as a restaurant or bar usually employing four artists or less. The format of this type of engagement normally requires soft music to facilitate the sale of cocktails or enhance the atmosphere in a restaurant. Included under the broad heading of lounge entertainers would be a solo violinist at an exclusive dinner club, all the way to a four-man country or rock group performing at a Saturday night "watering hole." There'll obviously be exceptions to this generalization in that some lounges may employ a group larger than four artists. Normally, however, a lounge will attempt to keep the number of artists employed to a minimum. Another characteristic of a lounge engagement is that the audiences are small. Generally this "stage" is not conducive to the performance of original material.

The lounge market employs thousands of artists, providing jobs for many individuals involved in the entertainment business on a part-time basis, or artists in the early stages of their career. Moreover, many artists who have become weary of the concert circuit or of larger clubs prefer the low-key environment and relaxed atmosphere of lounge engagements.

Rock and Show Rooms. The next club "stage" consists of rock and show rooms. Traditionally, these types of clubs have more of a music or dance-oriented atmosphere than do lounges. Because of the emphasis on music and dancing, these types of clubs are livelier than lounges. Consequently, the format may be more conducive to the performance of original material. Rock and show rooms usually employ groups of artists ranging from four to ten members. More emphasis is placed on using the popular entertainers from the local or regional area. For this reason the budget is usually larger than lounges. Popular rock and show groups aspiring to become recording acts can perform fifty-two weeks a year in all areas of the United States because of the abundance of these rooms. Almost every city of moderate size has at least one rock or show room. Surprisingly, many smaller cities have show rooms with high budgets.

We've purposely omitted discos from this survey of club "stages" because of their emphasis on recorded music as opposed to live entertainment. The discos that do utilize live music would be included in the rock and show room category.

Showcase or Listening Room. The showcase or listening room is another very important category of club, especially from the standpoint of the artist's career development. In many major cities, especially entertainment centers, there are key clubs that have a policy of only booking recording artists. The format and atmosphere is listening-oriented and is well suited to the presentation of original material. These clubs are usually well-covered by trade press reviewers from publications such as *Billboard, Record World, Cash Box,* and *Variety.* They are also well attended by the general press, industry figures, and members of the record-buying public. The potential for exposure and the concert-like atmosphere make this "stage" an extremely important place for breaking in a new recording artist.

Booking an artist in a showcase club can often be difficult because of the number of new artists trying to obtain bookings in these rooms. The manager should seek the help of the booking agent and record company to secure these dates. He should also be careful not to play a showcase club until the artist has sufficient personal appearance experience and a legitimate career development reason for playing the date.

The record company will often help subsidize the artist's appearances in showcase rooms through tour support, radio and print advertising buys, and so forth. This support is often necessary since the showcase club usually doesn't pay top dollar because of the competition factor among artists. Showcase or listening room dates can be a critical factor in a new artist's career.

Large Hotels and National Club Chains. The last "stage" available to the artist seeking to develop himself in the club market is large hotels and national club chains. This category includes hotels in large cities such as the Hilton or Hyatt chains, or the major hotels in Las Vegas,

Miami, and other resorts. It also encompasses large national chains such as the Playboy Clubs. Normally the budgets are very good in this segment of the club market. Because of their substantial entertainment allowances, these types of clubs are capable of attracting the superstars of the entertainment industry. There are no restrictions on the number of artists employed. From single performers to extravagant productions, the hotels and chains have the resources to buy the best. At this level, the artist's fees are high and so is the standard of artistic excellence.

These types of rooms serve several functions. Performers who may not have been tremendously successful in the recording aspect of their careers, but who are nonetheless super entertainers, find this level appealing and financially rewarding. Many hit recording artists also find this "stage" to be a lucrative source of income. Conversely, many artists who've had hit records but desire to limit the number of concert appearances also find this "stage" attractive.

This particular aspect of the club market is international in scope. Because of the global dimension of the large hotels, clubs, and restaurant chains, an international market has been created for artists entertaining on this level, provided their talent and performance has overseas appeal.

Private Parties
The second major category of live appearance is private parties. This level includes high school proms and dances, college fraternity parties, company parties, teen center dances, military base functions, and other private parties or dances utilizing live entertainment. This level of personal appearance offers the young artist numerous opportunities to develop and perfect his talent. Many national artists have come directly from this circuit. Colleges offer young artists the chance to build an extensive following long before a record affiliation is established. This following can be translated into future record sales.

This particular portion of the personal appearance market employs all types of artists (such as singles, groups, comedians, and duos). The format of most of these types of engagements is largely dance-oriented. The audiences are generally receptive and lively. It's a good market for the young artist in that it allows him to develop his stage presence and musical ability while also providing reasonably good compensation.

Concerts

The last broad heading of live appearances is the concert market. This segment can be broken down into two parts: college concerts and promotions.

College Concerts. Most every college, regardless of its size, presents concerts of some kind for its students during the school year. The college concert circuit is a good way to popularize or introduce new recording artists as well as maintain and expand the following of established acts. College audiences represent an important source for record sales. A recording artist and his manager should always be aware of the value of this market in terms of potential record sales. College concerts assimulate all types of artists with varying styles. Generally, the colleges allocate high budgets for concert entertainment. This aspect makes the market very attractive to artists with several hit records to their credit. The size of the audiences range from 1000 seat auditoriums to 15,000 seat colosseums. The colleges are frequent and consistent purchasers of concert entertainment.

Promotions. The other phase of concerts is promotions. Included in this category are independent promoters and promotion companies who book artists for an isolated concert promotion all the way to arranging a multicity cross-country tour. Whereas the college concert buyer isn't motivated to book an act based solely on the profit feasibility, the promoter is profit-oriented. It's his livelihood. Normally, the veteran promoter has established a relationship with various booking agents and managers of national artists. Once a promoter has proven himself financially sound and reliable, agents and managers entrust him with the promotion of more dates and subsequently entire tours. The promoter is the purchaser of entertainment. He'll sign the artist performance contract as employer, thus guaranteeing the artist's fee, arrange the location for the concert, promote the event, and coordinate the actual performance the night of the show. He must also make sure that the artist and all who participate in producing the show are paid, plus be responsible for applicable taxes associated with the production of the concert. He takes all the risk for a potential profit. With the rising prices of artists, arena, radio, printing, and amusement taxes, the promoter must select the artist he promotes cautiously. For this reason, the professional promoter will attempt to book complete tours in order to insulate himself from a fatal loss on a one-night promotion. Veteran promoters are primarily interested in the headliner acts and tour packages. The novice promoter usually gets the lesser known acts to promote. However, this is how a promoter develops his reputation. If he can help an agent, manager, or record company develop the market potential of a new artist by promoting a tour, and the artist subsequently becomes successful, he'll have gained their respect as a capable promoter. As a result, he's likely to get additional dates for the artist he helped to develop.

Many college students, who serve as entertainment buyers for their schools, establish friendships with booking agents and managers. Often, these college students prove themselves trustworthy and capable promoters. Consequently, the agents will sell them dates during the summer for their own entrepreneurial promotions. It must be emphasized that both booking agents and managers of national artists exercise the utmost caution when dealing with unknown promoters. The financial repercussions to agent, manager, and artist are simply too great to entrust a tour or a string of dates to a beginner. If a particular promotion isn't successful and the promoter doesn't have the financial capacity to cover the loss, who'll pay the artist? Take this isolated situation and multiply the loss times eight, ten, or fifteen cities in a tour! The artist could conceivably play a multi-city tour, and after paying motel, transportation, equipment rentals, and lose money. Even if the artist is protected by contract, the cost and time to litigate may make the collection process economically unfeasible. For these reasons, booking agents normally require substantial deposits from promoters. The economic consequences to the artist are simply too serious not to exercise extreme care in this area.

In some instances, a well-known artist will retain his own promoter to set the entire tour. This is possible when the artist is so popular and is in such demand that normal promotional efforts to insure a profitable show aren't needed. Despite this popularity, a local contact, in most cases, will still be utilized to coordinate necessary details. An artist desiring to set his own tour usually will have his own promoter or coordinator contact a local promoter and will pay him a flat fee for assisting in making the arrangements in certain cities. Under this approach, the local promoter doesn't risk his money, but just performs a task for a fee.

The size of promotions varies, but the more expensive attraction forces the promoter into a larger arena to make the show economically feasible. Generally, the professional promoter is concerned with concerts that have the capability of filling 5000 seats and up. The optimum promotion obviously depends on the artist, size of the city, arena, and overall cost considerations.

Recording artists utilize the concert appearance to promote record sales. Often, the record company will financially assist the artist and promoter by means of tour support to help generate popularity for its artist and his records. A successful performance in a stadium seating 50,000 people or an arena seating 20,000 can translate into significant record sales. For this reason, the major record companies feel that well-promoted, successful concert appearances by their artists are a must in their overall marketing program. The experienced manager, artist, and promoter recognize this and work closely with the record company when promoting a concert tour.

The Contract

The contracts used in booking artists for live appearances overlap as to terms and conditions, depending on the type of engagement involved. The name of employer, engagement location and address, date and time of engagement, rehearsal hours, and wage terms are all standard information contained in any artist performance contract. Also found in most contracts are clauses regarding the inability of the artist to perform due to sickness, accident, strikes, civil turmoil, epidemics, mechanical malfunctions, Acts of God, or conditions totally beyond the control of the artist. The American Federation of Musicians has a standard contract form used by all licensed affiliated booking agents. The beginning manager is well advised to familiarize himself with its terms.

The artist performing in the club market will frequently encounter clauses providing for room accommodations and discounts for food and beverages. These extra gratuities are sometimes essential in order to make some engagements economically feasible for the artist. The manager should insure that all the terms are contained in the performance contract to avoid any dispute during the engagement and to facilitate financial planning of the artist's tour. In the club market, it's also often necessary to set forth the exact hours of rehearsal time during the day in clubs that have constant customer traffic.

The basic performance contract for concerts, promotions, and private parties is very similar to the club contract. However, unusual features do occur in the contracts for college concerts and promotions. Many artists performing in these markets have certain additional requirements necessary for the successful presentation of their show. These extra requirements are contained in an attachment to the performance contract called a "rider."

Some riders are quite extensive and contain costly provisions for the employer. For instance, many artists require the employer to furnish a specific type of sound system that can cost several thousand dollars. In addition, musical equipment, room accommodations, and special transportation, as well as food and beverages, often appear as requirements in riders. The artist and manager must be cautious when preparing a rider so it does not take on the appearance of a scavanger hunt list. On the other hand, the employer should review the rider requirements carefully so as to be totally aware of all cost considerations relative to the purchase of a specific artist. An experienced booking agent will normally advise the purchaser of the requirements contained on the artist rider before a date is booked.

The artist performance contract for promotions will require that the price of tickets and number of available seats be included. Furthermore, the number of gratis seats is normally restricted. This occurs especially when the artist is to receive a guaranteed amount against a percentage of the total proceeds of ticket sales. Other clauses or terms pertaining to percentage of proceeds splits over a certain amount between artist and promoter are usually included.

The Booking Agency

The most direct way for an artist to secure club, private party, or concert engagements is through a booking agency. The booking agency serves as a meeting place for artists and purchasers of entertainment. Some agencies represent certain artists exclusively, thus requiring other agents to purchase from them if they have an engagement for that artist.

Booking agencies come in all sizes. There are a few that are international multidimensional firms, such as William Morris or ICM. They maintain offices in major cities throughout the world and have numerous departments representing entertainers, athletes, television personalities, authors, actors, and other types of celebrities.

The next strata of booking agencies are the ones specializing in musical entertainment: single artists, groups, and so forth. These types of companies can be further classified into club, private party, or concert-oriented agencies. There are hundreds of these types of firms in the United States providing service to the artist and entertainment buyer.

The manager should select a booking agent capable of securing the type of engagements best suited to the development of the artist's career. The first step is for manager and artist to determine on what "stage" the artist should appear. Once this determination has been made, there are literally hundreds of agents to choose from. Finding the best agent for an artist may turn into a trial-and-error process. The manager must be alert and cautiously watch over the artist-agent relationship.

Agent fees generally range from 10% to 20%. Normally an agent's fee for booking a club engagement is 10% while the fee for a private party or concert ranges from 10% to 20%. The fees for booking are somewhat negotiable, depending on the strength of the artist and the service the artist requires.

The American Federation of Musicians has an exclusive Agent Artist Agreement, which attempts to govern this relationship between its members and affiliated agents. While the agreement covers broad areas of an exclusive agent-artist relationship, there are usually certain specialized terms associated with each situation. These special twists should be incorporated into the agreement.

As we will discuss in a later chapter, the agent can be a valuable factor in the development of the artist's career. The manager and artist should cultivate their relationship with agents, encouraging their comments and criticisms throughout the artist's career.

17.
Merchandising, Commercials, and Endorsements

Although record and songwriting royalties and personal appearance fees comprise the bulk of most of an artist's income, he also stands to gain from merchandising, commercials, and endorsements. Certain celebrities have commanded fees or received royalties totaling more than a million dollars from these ancillary sources. The continued development of the modern media and the refinement of mass-marketing techniques, combined with the increasing importance and influence of entertainment figures, will no doubt continue to enhance potential earnings in these areas. An astute manager, aware of the possibilities that exist in these fields can help raise his artist's income level and make effective use of these vehicles for promotion and image-projection purposes.

Merchandising
One area of ancillary income and name projection that has become critically important in the last decade is merchandising. "Merchandising" generally refers to the marketing of products to the public on the strength of the artist's name or likeness. These products can include T-shirts, souvenir photograph books, posters, dolls, toys, and games. The range of products possible is limited only by

the imagination. For example, there have been Elton John pinball machines and Dolly Parton dolls.

Merchandising usually involves a licensing agreement whereby the artist assigns to a merchandising specialist the right to use his name and likeness in connection with the design, manufacture, and sale of certain products. In return for this right, the merchandiser will pay the artist a fee or royalty which is often based on a percentage of retail sales. The amount payable to the artist will depend on such factors as the scope and term of the license, exclusivity or non-exclusivity, popularity and appeal of the artist, and the type of product or products to be merchandised.

The artist has several alternatives in the area of merchandising. He may either grant full or partial rights to a merchandiser as previously suggested, or he can retain certain or all of such rights and handle the merchandising himself. Except for certain limited items, the artist is probably best advised to enter into an agreement with an experienced merchandising company set up to do an effective job in this area. There are a number of specialists in the field located throughout the country, depending on the scope of the merchandising campaign.

Besides the points just stated, when negotiating a merchandising agreement, the artist and his manager will want to include a provision giving them the right of approval of all projects to be undertaken. This would include not only the type of product to be produced, but also any artwork, design, or copy associated with the product, as well as specific marketing techniques to be employed. Without this clause, the artist and manager run the risk of losing control over the artist's image development. A distasteful product or indiscriminate development of products could have a disastrous effect on his career. Such products have the potential for overexposing the artist or creating negative reactions in the eyes of the public. This can translate into decreased record sales and lessening of demand for personal appearances.

Even assuming the product is desirable and consistent with the artist's image, distasteful or inappropriate advertising or other marketing devices and techniques could still create negative reactions.

The key to effective merchandising is to give the public a product they want and to present it so as to enhance the artist's popularity rather than to diminish it. This is not always an easy task. Good taste and thoughtful planning should serve as primary guidelines for any merchandising campaign.

The new artist negotiating his first record contract should be especially conscious of the potential value of his name and likeness. Many record companies will try to secure exclusive merchandising rights from the artist in return for a royalty based on the net sums they receive. The percentage is usually 50%. The manager should try to retain these rights, at least in areas not bearing on promotion of his records. For instance, it might be advantageous for the artist to give non-exclusive merchandising rights to the label in specific areas that could be used to promote record sales, such as T-shirts and posters. However, toys, dolls, and games would generally be outside the scope of legitimate record-promotion tools. If rights are granted, the artist and manager should retain all rights of approval mentioned earlier.

As with record companies, the artist should not give merchandising rights to specialists in the field until the artist's career merits such an arrangement. There's always the danger that a premature grant of rights can result in less favorable contract terms for the artist because of lack of bargaining strength. However, when the artist's career has reached such a level, the artist and manager should carefully consider the consequences before committing themselves to a merchandising campaign.

Commercials

Commercials comprise another important source of income and provide the artist with a vehicle for exposure. Entertainment personalities of star caliber can command fees in the six figures for a national advertising campaign. They can also be expected to be seen by millions through television, radio, and magazine exposure. However, just as with everything else, there's the potential for damage to an artist's career if the manager's dealings with the "commerical" market are not handled properly.

The word " commercial" may encompass any means by which an artist is used to promote, advertise, and sell a product. It may take the form of an on-camera television spot or a voice-over on a radio jingle. In other instances, the commercial may be a printed advertisement in a national magazine or may even involve using the artist's picture on outdoor billboards or in connection with in-store product displays. In the case of a comprehensive national campaign, all of these different formats may be used.

Just as a commercial can take many forms, so it can be aimed at specific markets. It can be targeted at national, regional, or local markets. All of these variables will have a bearing on the desirability of the particular commercial and the money the artist can hope to make in return for his services.

Most major national advertisers retain advertising agencies who have the responsibility for developing and producing their advertising campaigns. When developing a campaign that will call for the use of an entertainment personality, the agency will usually contact the major, multifaceted booking or talent agencies and other smaller agents with access to important national acts. As a general rule, these agencies are based either in New York or on the West Coast. Since the advertising agencies' area of expertise is not entertainment, they depend on the agents' knowledge and experience in the field.

In some instances, an agency will have an in-house music department that might have contacts directly with artists, managers, producers, and record companies. In this case, the advertising agency might choose to deal directly with the artist or his personal representative.

The best way for a manager to get his artist commercial work, if he has no advertising contacts of his own, is to develop a relationship with an agent who regularly works in the commercial field. It may often be possible, depending on bargaining position, for the manager to work with one agent for personal appearances and another for commercial work.

Basically, there are two approaches to advertising. One is "product sell." This consists of using the artist to make a direct appeal to the consumer to buy the sponsor's product. The other approach is known as "image advertising." This is a more indirect concept. Here, there is no effort to make a direct sale. The advertising agency appeals to the buyer by suggesting their product is a desirable commodity that should be a part of the consumer's lifestyle. Many national advertisers use this form of advertising in their national campaigns to supplement a local "product sell" approach. Image advertising is generally well suited for entertainers because of their mass appeal to large numbers of people. The key here is to tie the product to the artist, thereby taking advantage of the artist's popularity.

When a campaign calls for use of an entertainer, the agency will usually come up with a type of person who would fit what they're doing. For example, let's suppose the agency wanted to do an image advertising television commerical for a soft drink manufacturer. The largest target group of buyers of this product consists of preteens, teenagers, and young adults. The commercial is designed to center around an attractive female, album-oriented MOR/soft rock recording artist in her mid-twenties to early thirties. The agency will draw up a list of five or six singers who fit this description and the general budget range they have to work with. The advertising agency will then contact agents to inquire about an artist's interest and availability. Generally speaking, advertising agencies don't work with much lead time. Often, an artist's unavailability will end his chance of doing the commercial because air dates, *once they're set,* are usually inflexible. Once the agency finds an artist who fits their requirements, a contract is negotiated and a production schedule is set.

Deciding Whether or Not to Accept the Commercial.
There are a number of factors an artist or manager should

consider when determining whether to accept or reject a commercial. Naturally, the money involved must be sufficient to warrant involvement by the artist. There's also the consideration of how a commercial will affect the artist's image and career development. Many factors have a bearing on this question. First of all, what product is to be advertised? It must not be inconsistent with the artist's image. For instance, an artist with a reputation for an unorthodox lifestyle would probably not want to do a bank commercial. A beer commercial wouldn't be appropriate for an artist sporting an All-American, wholesome image. The product should likewise not be the kind that would create negative reactions, such as a deodorant or foot product.

The terms of the contract to be negotiated with the advertising agency also will bear on whether the artist should accept the commercial. For instance, an artist should avoid a long-term commitment unless the financial return is sufficient. The artist may not want to grant unlimited rights to use his likeness in things such as in-store displays, posters, and billboards, arguing this would cheapen his career.

Another point to consider is the effect a commercial will have on the artist's future worth in the commercial market. Every time an artist does a commercial, his value diminishes. This is especially true if the campaign is national in scope. Eventually, he'll no longer be fresh and unique. Also, sponsors and agencies prefer to use a personality not closely connected with another product. Therefore, a manager, hoping for a more lucrative contract, may want to defer accepting any commercial offer until later in the artist's career. Or, he may want to think about a regional commercial to gain experience and some financial return without running as great a risk of lessening his artist's value.

A manager should be especially wary of the danger of overexposure. Too many television guest shots, coupled with an extensive national advertising campaign, could result in oversaturation. Consequently, demand for the artist's concert performances and records might fall off, severely damaging his career. No commercial is worth taking if it will have an extreme negative effect on a developing career. By the same token, a well-produced national television commercial for a good product can give an artist's career a significant boost.

In short, the proper degree of exposure is a question of judgment. The manager must make a calculated projection of a commercial's effect based on all relevant information at his disposal.

Negotiating the Contract. Some of the more important factors to be considered in the negotiation process are the length of the contract and date from which the term will be measured. For example, assume a television commercial is to run for one year. Should the year begin running from the date the contract is signed, or from the date of the first production of the commercial, or from first date of airing? This is a negotiable point. Other key terms include territory: national, regional, or local airing. Scope of rights, such as television rights only, television and radio, print, outdoor advertising, and point of purchase (which includes in-store displays and posters). In addition, advances, guarantees or flat fee, and creative control of production are other points that must be negotiated.

Normally, an artist is paid on the basis of either an advance against residuals or a guarantee of residual remuneration based on a negotiated percentage of applicable AFTRA (American Federation of Television and Radio Artists) or SAG (Screen Actors Guild) scale. Depending on bargaining position, an artist's manager may negotiate a contract that pays the artist at the rate of scale, double scale, or higher. This rate is then multiplied by the number of radio and/or television airings the commercial receives according to AFTRA and/or SAG rate schedules, and is paid to the artist in much the same way a songwriter is paid by performing right societies. The manager should become familiar with AFTRA and SAG rates, rules, and procedures. Representatives of these organizations will be glad to talk to managers about their respective organizations.

In the area of commercials, timing can mean everything.

The manager should make sure a commercial will have either a positive career development effect or will provide the artist with substantial income. But an artist should never damage his image or sacrifice his career development for the sake of the money he can earn from doing a commercial. By the same token, the right commercial at the right stage of an artist's career can be beneficial careerwise as well as financially.

Endorsements

A third major area of ancillary income is from endorsements. This area has many of the attributes of merchandising and commercials. It involves the artist's name and likeness being directly connected with a specially manufactured product line. Professional athletes serve as a frequent example of endorsements, such as Mickey Mantle bats, Johnny Miller menswear, or Chris Evert tennis rackets. Endorsements are also available to entertainers for a variety of products. The same basic considerations discussed in merchandising and commercials also apply to endorsements.

Another form of endorsement often available to athletes and actors and to a lesser extent recording artists is the spokesmanship. Here, the artist is retained as the exclusive spokesman and public relations representative for a particular industry, association or company. These agreements usually involve multi-year commitments for very substantial amounts sometimes in excess of one million dollars. This would encompass such areas as national media advertising campaigns, product endorsements, interviews, personal appearances at sales outlets, and industry or company conventions.

As mentioned earlier, the price a sponsor is willing to pay is directly proportional to the celebrity's "star" value, image, and previous commercial exposure. Many managers may resist commercial offers, holding out for a more lucrative spokesmanship package at a later stage of the artist's career. This is always a gamble because a manager can never be sure that an artist will be able to sustain his career over a long period of time or, even if he does, that a spokes-manship offer will be made. On the other hand, many art-ists would never consider a spokesmanship, feeling that they'd be selling out their artistic principles. As with com-mercials, the right strategy is a decision that will vary from artist to artist, depending on his particular set of cir-cumstances.

Summary
The fields of merchandising, commercials and endorse-ments provide the artist with another avenue to financial fulfillment. But they can also present some very tricky deci-sions for the artist and his manager. The rule in this area is to think twice before making a commitment.

18.
International Considerations

During the past fifteen years, the entertainment industry has witnessed the unprecedented growth of international markets. This has had a significant impact on the earnings of United States based record companies, music publishers, and artists. These markets now account for a substantial share of gross income earned by these various entertainment entities.

In 1974, *The International Buyers Guide* published by *Billboard* magazine estimated that the United States accounted for approximately 42% of all retail record sales in the world market. The remaining 58% of sales were distributed throughout the rest of the world as follows: Europe 32%, Japan 14%, Latin America 4.5%, Australia 2.5%, and Africa 1%. These figures are sure to increase as more nations of the world achieve a higher standard of living, acquire more leisure time, and continue to improve and be served by the communications network.

More artists than ever before are thinking in international terms. The popularity and interest in American artists has never been greater. This favorable situation presents the artist and manager with the opportunity to broaden their appeal and increase their incomes.

The acceptance around the world of artists' records or

songs with truly international appeal can make a big difference in a record company or music publisher's annual balance sheet. For example, the American disco hit "Rock Your Baby," recorded by George McCrae in 1974, reached the record charts of 51 countries, often achieving the number-one position. Artists such as Abba or Shirley Bassey are top draws throughout the world. These artists enjoy the same type of global popularity that many artists receive only in their own country.

Foreign Record Sales

One important aspect of the world entertainment market that should be considered by the artist and his manager is record sales. Generally, when an artist signs with a major American record company, the label will demand world rights to the artist's recordings. In the case of some few major artists, certain territories may possibly be exempted.

Foreign record sales are usually achieved in one of two ways. Either through major American record companies, such as CBS and RCA, which have affiliated companies in the major developed nations of the world. These companies license master rights to their foreign branch affiliates. Or through other American companies without branch affiliates who enter into licensing agreements with foreign record labels. These agreements can either take the form of a blanket worldwide foreign agreement with a major overseas company that has its own branch affiliates such as London-based E.M.I., or they can be on a country-by-country basis with independent companies.

As a general rule, an artist is paid a royalty calculated at 50% of the rate normally paid for American sales. This rate may be negotiated up to as much as 75% of the domestic rate, depending on the artist's bargaining position and whether or not the American record company is dealing with its affiliated branches or unaffiliated independent licensees. This reduced rate is justified by the record company because it receives substantially less on foreign sales than on domestic sales.

Most recording contracts make no guarantees as to release of the artist's records in foreign markets. Depending on bargaining position, the artist should try to negotiate a guaranteed release of his records in key countries of the world, especially if the record company insists on securing world rights. But he must be prepared for the record company's reply to this type of proposal. They may say that they don't always have control over what will be released in a given country, especially if independent licensees are employed. Another frequent argument they offer is that the foreign record company won't want to release a record in their territory unless it's either a hit in the United States or unless the artist has a previous track record in the particular foreign country.

The status of foreign record deals may be somewhat different where the artist is signed to an independent producer who, in turn, deals with the U.S. record company. An established producer may succeed in exempting certain foreign territories from his contract with the American company. In this event, the producer would be free to make his own licensing agreements on a country-by-country basis in return for an aggregate producer/artist royalty.

The manager interested in expanding his artist's career into international markets should investigate the overseas capabilities of various foreign record labels as one consideration in choosing an American company. Some domestic companies are more conscious of international sales than others. Larger companies with foreign affiliates may be in a better position to release and promote records in foreign territories. By the same token, a smaller company with strong independent licensees may be able to devote more time to help the artist promote record sales in foreign territories.

Consideration should also be given to the type of material the artist records. Manager, artist, and producer should seek songs with international appeal. However, they should be careful not to think internationally at the expense of the American market. This would be self-defeating, especially since many major countries look to success of a record in the United States as an indication of whether it will be released in a foreign market. The goal here is to strike a balance between domestic and foreign appeal.

As we've seen earlier, success in music publishing is tied largely to the success of commercial recordings of published works. This rule applies equally to foreign territories.

Agreements With Subpublishers

The essence of foreign music publishing involves agreements between American publishers and their affiliated or independent overseas licensees. These contractual relationships are referred to as "subpublishing agreements." An American publisher will enter into these agreements much in the same manner as an American record company enters into foreign record licensing agreements. Typically, an American publisher will grant rights on either a song-by-song or catalog basis to foreign music publishers for a negotiated term. The subpublisher will seek to exploit and promote the compositions and collect and account for income received. As compensation, the foreign publisher will retain a percentage of earnings derived from the commercial usage of the material. Depending on the commercial potential of a particular composition or catalog, the foreign subpublisher may pay the copyright owner an advance against royalties to obtain rights to the material.

Generally, no provision is made in the songwriter contract for payment of a reduced royalty on foreign income to the writer. However, as a practical matter, a writer's income will be diminished because his royalty is based on a percentage of income actually received by the publisher. Since the foreign subpublisher deducts a percentage of the gross income he collects, there'll be less money to divide between the publisher and writer. For instance, let's assume $100 in mechanical royalties is earned in France. Assuming the French publisher by contract is entitled to 50% of all mechanicals earned in the territory, he'll retain $50 and remit the remaining $50 to the American publisher. The American publisher will, in turn, normally be obligated to pay the writer 50% of all mechanical income actually collected by him. Consequently, $25 is payable to the writer and $25 is retained by the publisher.

It should be noted here that most subpublishing agreements grant the foreign licensee the right to collect all mechanical, synchronization, and miscellaneous income. With regard to performances, the subpublisher either collects the total publisher's share or just the foreign publisher's share of performances directly from the foreign performing rights society. Generally, the foreign society will collect the writer's share of performing income as a result of reciprocal agreements with ASCAP and BMI. The writer's share is paid directly to the respective American society after deduction of a small collection fee. The American society will pay the applicable amount directly to the writer.

A major consideration of the writer/artist when signing with an American publisher is a determination of whether royalties paid to the company by foreign subpublishers and ultimately to him are computed at the source and are not diminished on account of any sublicense granted by the subpublisher. For instance, let's assume the American publisher enters into a subpublishing agreement with a French publisher for the territories of France and Switzerland. The subpublisher negotiates a clause whereby it agrees to pay the original publisher 50% of the income actually received by it in France. The French publisher doesn't have an office in Switzerland and thus finds it necessary to enter into a subpublishing agreement of its own with a Swiss publisher on a 50% royalty basis. The money earned by the Swiss publisher is $100. The division of income in this situation would be as follows: $50 is retained by the Swiss publisher, with the balance being remitted to the French publisher. The French publisher in turn retains 50% or $25 and remits the balance to the original American publisher. Out of this $25, $12.50 is remitted to the writer, and the balance is retained by the American publisher.

Sometimes, these types of sublicenses are unavoidable, especially in order to insure representation in smaller countries or where the original publisher is in a disadvantageous bargaining position. However, whenever possible, the writer should determine the American publisher's foreign subpublishing structure and whether payments are computed at the source from the important foreign territories.

Usually, the American publisher will have absolute discretion as to the terms it negotiates with regard to foreign licensing or subpublishing agreements. This right will, of course, be subject to any limitations in its agreement with the writer. The writer can protect himself from improvident foreign agreements in one of two ways. The first is through a restriction in the original writer's contract which may be difficult to obtain. The second method is to choose a domestic publisher with an active and successful subpublishing situation.

Translations, Adaptations, and Arrangements
Another aspect of foreign publishing that can affect the artist/writer is the right of the subpublisher to make translations, adaptations, and arrangements of his compositions, including the right to have new lyrics written. Without this right, it would be extremely difficult to exploit the writer's songs in certain territories. Royalties payable to a local lyric writer will vary depending on local industry practice and the strength of the lyricist. It's customary for the subpublisher to pay the lyric writer royalties based on the mechanical and synchronization uses and sales of printed editions out of its share of the income. The local lyric writer's share of performing rights income will come from the American lyric writer's share. In some cases, foreign arrangers may be entitled to receive a small portion of the American composer's performance share.

As with records, the artist/writer should be aware of the adaptability and appeal his songs will have in foreign territories. It's the responsibility of the foreign subpublisher to seek recordings by artists in the foreign territories. In order to do this, the subpublisher must have material that will be acceptable to these artists. Because of language differences in non-English-speaking countries, melody becomes a key consideration in adaptability. The writer interested in international acceptance of his material is well advised to acquaint himself with the musical tastes of some of the key foreign markets, such as the United Kingdom, France, Germany, and Japan. Often a writer may write with a certain artist in mind. As we have seen earlier in the chapter, a successful recording by an artist with an international following can not only account for considerable income from the foreign territories but can also help develop the composition into an international standard that will be recorded literally hundreds of times over the life of the copyright.

Personal Appearances

A third major area of international concern is the personal appearance. As in the United States, concert, nightclub, radio, and television appearances provide a lucrative source of income, while also being an effective record promotion tool. The same rules regarding coordination of personal appearances and recording company promotion apply equally to the foreign market. The large booking agencies such as William Morris and I.C.M. have foreign offices to handle the booking of a foreign tour. Smaller agencies often maintain reciprocal working agreements with foreign agencies. If the artist is not affiliated with an agency that has international connections, the manager can contact reputable foreign agents or consultants who specialize in helping arrange overseas tours.

A popular American artist can command substantial fees in certain foreign markets while also helping to boost record sales and accompanying music-publishing income. The same general principles dealing with the personal appearance and the road apply to foreign tours. Certainly the manager and road manager should place special emphasis on each respective country's laws and regulations relating to passports, visas, work permits, and any other potential travel restrictions.

If the artist is to travel to non-English-speaking countries, thought should be given to hiring interpreters or guides to help insure that the tour goes smoothly. It's helpful for the manager, artist, and support personnel to have at least some familiarization with the geography, culture, and customs of the countries they'll be visiting. This will not only contribute to a more successful tour but will add to the enjoyment of the experience by the artist and his traveling contingent. The local agent, record company, or music publisher can often provide the artist and manager with help in this area.

Besides providing a vehicle to expand the artist's markets, the foreign tour is an excellent device that can be used to avoid domestic overexposure. An absence of several months from an artist's home country can often help create a renewed demand for the artist once he resumes domestic touring.

Summary

As the world economy improves and technological developments continue, it seems to be a safe bet that the demand for quality entertainment on a global scale will continue to increase. The astute artist and manager should strive to help fill this demand through internationally oriented career planning.

Part IV
Career Maintenance and Control

19.
The Manager's Juggling Act

What does a manager do? Or better yet, what doesn't he do? Generally speaking, a manager does anything necessary to further the career of his artist-client. He's a coordinator, advisor, negotiator, psychologist, planner, promoter and a friend to the artist. We believe the term "juggler" aptly describes his many diverse functions and responsibilities. Just as one problem is solved, new ones requiring immediate attention usually appear. Management is an ongoing process with no real stopping point short of termination of the artist-manager relationship. The manager must be aware of all aspects of the artist's career. He's the pivot point for literally hundreds of decisions that must be made daily. The manager's ability to make the proper decision at the right time will greatly enhance the success of the artist's career. On the other hand, his failure to act in a timely manner as daily problems unfold can severely damage the artist's career development.

The best way to define the manager's duties and responsibilities is to construct a typical day in the life of the artist's manager.

The day begins, as in any other business office, with the opening of the morning mail. The manager finds several artists' performance contracts included in the stack of correspondence. He carefully reviews each contract, giving special attention to the date, time, and place of engagement, and the compensation clauses. If deposit checks are enclosed with any of the contracts, the proper accounting entries must be made and the checks deposited in the artist's bank account. If the artist's accountant maintains the financial books, then the checks will be processed according to the predetermined accounting procedure. If the manager finds anything in the contracts that doesn't meet his approval, he'll contact the booking agent regarding the appropriate modifications. However, on this particular morning, all the contracts received are in order, so he promptly signs each one and instructs his secretary to return the remaining copies to the booking agent.

Also included in the mail are offers for live performances received by the booking agent. Each offer must be examined in view of its economic, exposure, and routing value. The manager will normally contact the artist if any offer has unusual features. The manager notices one of the engagement offers is for an amount twice the artist's normal asking price. However, the engagement is to be held outdoors. The artist and manager had previously formulated several live-performance guidelines, one being no outdoor engagements. Since the money offered is extremely high, and several other name attractions have already agreed to perform at this engagement, the artist might want to consider this offer. Knowing the artist's daily schedule, the manager decides to contact him later on in the afternoon about this matter.

After the mail has been processed, the manager begins making and returning telephone calls. Representatives from the artist's record label, publishing company, and booking agency have all called requesting various information. These people must receive top priority. Upon returning the record company's call, the manager is surprised to learn that the artist's album is selling well in four new markets. Excited by this information, the manager calls the booking agent, giving him this information. He informs the agent of his desire for the artist to perform in these new markets. The agent advises the manager that he'll check with buyers in the new markets and will be back in touch toward the end of the day.

Before making any further telephone calls, the manager is interrupted by an unannounced visitor—the artist. In short order, the manager learns the artist is very upset with one of the members of his backup group. With the fall tour just a few weeks off, the artist is pessimistic about being ready in time unless something can be done about the attitude of this particular musician. The manager attempts to get all the facts so he can define the real problem. Is it the musician's playing or singing ability? Is it his attitude? Or is there a personality conflict? What's the real problem? After an in-depth discussion, the manager feels he knows what the trouble is and how to remedy it. He reassures the artist that the problem will be solved and encourages him to make the most out of today's rehearsal. An appointment is set with the musician for later that afternoon. Before the artist leaves, the manager asks him about the offer for the outdoor engagement. The artist's answer is, "No!"

After the artist leaves, the manager is informed that he has an emergency telephone call from the artist's public relations firm. Trouble! The firm can't have the publicity campaign ready in time to correspond with the artist's tour. The manager and public relations man have a rather heated discussion regarding the firm's inefficient handling of the artist's affairs. The manager has had enough excuses and delays. He terminates the relationship with the publicity firm. Immediately following this unfortunate encounter, the manager instructs his secretary to arrange appointments with representatives of three other public relations firms for the next day. Time is running out. The artist's publicity campaign must be planned and activated immediately in order to coincide with the efforts of the record company for promoting the upcoming tour.

Next the manager receives a call from the booking agent who informs him he has secured firm offers from a promoter for all of the new markets mentioned by the record company. However, the promoter wants to block-book the dates for several thousand dollars less than the normal price. The manager instructs the booking agent to have the buyer submit his offer in written form. The agent says he'll call back when a telegram is received.

The manager contacts the promotion department at the record company to inquire about the feasibility of the label providing extra tour support in the new markets to help off-set the lower live performance fee if he should accept the dates as offered. The record company representative tells the manager he'll check and be back in touch.

Lunchtime! Today the manager has a luncheon appointment scheduled with the artist's attorney. During the meeting, the attorney advises that all the employment agreements with the roadcrew now being used should be modified to include several new clauses. Moreover, the lease agreements for the tour vehicles have been approved and are ready for the artist's signature. In addition, the attorney explains the legal ramifications of an incident involving the artist and an irate auditorium manager at a concert performance earlier in the year. It seems that the artist became enraged at the way the auditorium manager's staff was handling the lighting effects and made some derogatory comments to the audience regarding the intellectual capacity of the crew. As a result, the auditorium manager is suing the artist for slander. Finally, the attorney presents the manager with the proceeds of a recent collection suit, which was successfully concluded, involving an overdue concert fee. All in all, the meeting wasn't too bad. The manager has experienced far worse.

The manager hurries back to the office to meet with the artist's producer. They're scheduled to review the artist's latest recordings. Both the manager and artist agree that the mixes on the recordings are terrible. Unfortunately, the manager must relay this information to the producer in such a way as to not upset him. The manager conveys the negative feelings of his client to the producer as tactfully as possible. After a lengthy session, the producer leaves convinced the manager is an idiot when it comes to recording and doesn't understand how the artist could put up with such incompetence. Nonetheless, the recordings will be re-mixed.

Immediately following the meeting with the producer, the booking agent calls with several new offers. After listening carefully, the manager accepts two of them, since they correspond with the tour's routing. Several of the offers merit consideration if the price can be increased or the dates changed. The remaining offers don't make sense from a routing or financial standpoint and are refused.

As the afternoon draws on, the road manager arrives to begin finalizing motel and travel accommodations for the tour. After discussing the budget limitations for these expense items, he begins making the necessary arrangements. The manager instructs him to contact the program directors at the important radio stations in the cities where engagements have been set in an effort to increase airplay for the artist's latest record. The manager sends the road manager into the adjoining office to start accumulating the necessary information to commence the in-house promotion campaign for the tour.

The manager next speaks with the artist's accountant regarding the bookkeeping procedure for the tour. The same system that has been previously employed will be used. The manager arranges a meeting between the accountant and road manager so they can discuss any questions he might have about the system.

Emergency call! The artist is at rehearsal and is in a rage. The monitors of the sound system aren't working. There'll be no rehearsal until they're fixed. The manager immediately locates a repairman and replacement equipment and has the road manager personally direct him to the rehearsal location.

Fifteen minutes later, the manager meets with the musician with whom the artist is experiencing problems. The manager learns that the musician is having some serious domestic difficulties. After a candid conversation, the manager is very sympathetic to the musician's situation. However, he explains the great pressure the artist is under due to the immediacy of the upcoming tour and the amount of rehearsal still to be done. The manager assures the musician he'll explain his situation to the artist and will encourage him to be understanding. Since the musician is quite concerned about several legal aspects of the situation, he advises the musician to see an attorney for counsel.

The manager calls the artist and tells him the results of the meeting with the musician. The artist is most understanding of the situation and is quite relieved to learn that the problem isn't being caused by some personality clash between him and the musician. However, the artist is still concerned over the sound system that still hasn't been repaired. The manager assures him that the road manager will take care of it.

Half an hour later, after solving the minor catastrophy with the sound system, the road manager returns and begins contacting radio-station program directors. The manager joins the road manager in talking to these people about the artist's upcoming appearance in their city. He enjoys playing the role of radio promotion man, especially after two stations promise to program the record.

Toward the end of the day, the booking agent informs the manager that firm offers have been received on the proposed engagements in the new market areas. Putting the agent on hold, the manager contacts the record company's Promotion Department to see if a decision has been made on extra tour-support money. The proposal is being considered by the Business Affairs Department. The manager advises the agent to delay the buyer until a decision can be made by the record company. Maybe they'll get an answer tomorrow.

That evening, the manager is scheduled to attend the artist's rehearsal to review a portion of the concert presentation being prepared for the upcoming tour. Watching and listening to the rehearsal stimulates the manager's thought patterns and images about his client. He has several comments and ideas to offer about the show being rehearsed. This is the area where manager and artist excel—they feed off each other's ideas. The manager's thoughts provoke additional ideas from the artist. After an hour-long discussion, both artist and manager are excited about several new approaches to the live performance they've agreed to try. They're both starting to feel the excitement of the upcoming tour.

Before leaving the artist's rehearsal, the manager again mentions the offer for the outdoor engagement. He asks the artist to reconsider because of the money involved and the positive exposure value. The manager also adds the fact that several other name recording artists will also be performing at the same concert. The artist agrees to think about it and give the manager an answer within the week.

The manager starts to leave, when he's cornered by two members of the artist's backup band who inquire about the itinerary for the tour. The manager briefs them of the general tour schedule and promises to give them an exact itinerary as soon as the details have been finalized.

On his way home, the manager can't help but think about the problems involved with finding a new public relations firm and activating a campaign in time for the tour. He also makes a mental note to call the record company tomorrow morning about his tour-support proposal. The conversation with the producer also pops into his mind. The manager smiles to himself, knowing the new tapes are going to be re-mixed, even though the producer thinks he has a tin ear. All the problems of the day are balanced out by the excitement generated by the rehearsal. The creative give and take with the artist make all the problems worth putting up with.

The manager arrives home late. He checks with his answering service for any calls. There's an urgent message to call the booking agent at home. The message has the making of another emergency.

The booking agent tells the manager that he's heard a rumor that the artist has been nominated as Best New Artist of the Year by an influential national magazine. The agent points out that this could dramatically raise the artist's asking price for personal appearances on the upcoming tour.

After hanging up, the manager's mind begins to race, thinking of all the implications and repercussions such a turn of events could have on his client's career. The excitement builds for the second time that evening. The manager must either confirm or deny the message that the booking agent has given him. He decides to call a friend on the West Coast who may know something about the report. It's almost midnight, but because of the time difference, it's only 9:00 PM in Los Angeles. He picks up the telephone for the thirtieth time since the beginning of the day and begins dialing a phone number scribbled on the back of one of his business cards. "Hello, Marc? I've just gotten a report that. . . ."

20.
Helping the Record Company Help You

Once the artist and manager have succeeded in establishing an affiliation with a major record company, they've cleared a crucial hurdle. In one way, they've finally achieved the success they worked so hard to attain. Yet in another, the work has only begun. Signing a contract with a viable record label and becoming an established recording artist are two entirely different things. To bridge this gap takes the same type of hard work it did to interest the company in the artist and negotiate the contract. The only difference now is that the record company is there to help you.

In order to maximize the artist's potential at this stage of his career, we feel that active, experienced management is an absolute necessity. Many self-managed acts will find it increasingly difficult to continue to develop their own careers once this level of success is attained. Nowhere is this more true than in the artist's relationship with his record company.

The record business today is highly sophisticated and potentially very lucrative. The manager's role in the ultimate success or failure of an artist's record career has become increasingly important. He's the artist's personal representative in all dealings involving the label. He acts as the artist's advocate, press secretary, advisor, planner,

BUSINESS REPLY CARD

FIRST CLASS   Permit No. 46048   NEW YORK, N.Y.

Postage will be paid by

Watson-Guptill Publications
1515 Broadway
New York, New York 10036

May we have your comments on

SUCCESSFUL ARTIST MANAGEMENT
by X.M. Frascogna, Jr., and H. Lee Hetherington

WE HOPE THAT YOU HAVE ENJOYED THIS BOOK AND THAT IT WILL OCCUPY A PROUD PLACE IN YOUR LIBRARY. WE WILL BE MOST GRATEFUL IF YOU WILL FILL OUT AND MAIL THIS CARD TO US.

Your comments: _____

_____

_____

How did this book come to your attention? _____

Bought at: _____   Gift: _____

Your business or profession: _____

Would you care to receive a catalog of our new publications?

☐ Yes   ☐ No

Name _____

Address _____

City _____   State _____   Zip Code _____

negotiator, decisionmaker, protector, and spokesman all rolled into one where the record company is concerned. He can be instrumental in helping the label allocate its resources and make the most effective use of its assets to break the artist from a record-sales standpoint. The artist simply doesn't have enough hours in his day to devote to the many and varied management duties and responsibilities involved in dealing with the record company.

The most common complaint against managers voiced by the record company executives we surveyed is that many of them don't fully understand or appreciate the function, structure, and inner workings of the record business in general and the record company in particular. On the other hand, they were quick to praise those professionals possessing this valuable knowledge and experience. Effective management is impossible unless the manager is able to relate to the record company on its own terms. This means he must have the same degree of competence, knowledge, and skill as those he'll be working with at the label.

Understanding Record Company Operations
The record company has one objective—to sell records. Record companies in the United States don't receive performance royalties from broadcasters as some do in Europe and other foreign territories. They don't share in income from the artist's concerts, television appearances, commercials, endorsements, or songwriting royalties. The only way they can make a profit and stay in business is by selling records. The manager should always keep this basic premise in mind. Any suggestion and request he makes should in some way be designed to help the record company succeed in their objective. The fact that the manager's plans and requests will also directly benefit the artist's career is of no real concern as long as it will help sell records.

Besides understanding the objective or purpose of the record company, the manager should also have a thorough understanding of the organizational structure and procedures of the label.

Most major record companies in the United States are based in recording centers such as Los Angeles or New York. Many have branch offices in other cities to deal with specific or specialized functions. For example, many labels maintain self-contained offices in Nashville that specialize in country music. Others maintain branches in key geographic locations around the country to handle regional marketing, promotion, and distribution.

Record companies are no different from other businesses. Most are divided into departments charged with jurisdiction over certain phases of the company's activities. Each department has a department head who reports to the president or other upper echelon executive. The president, in turn, reports to the board of directors, who are charged with the overall direction of the company.

Although no two companies are structured exactly alike, most are organized along the same lines with regard to division of responsibility according to subject matter. Each label has a chief executive officer and executive staff. They're charged with the overall operation and management of the label. Individual areas of responsibility are usually divided into the following departmental areas: Business Affairs; Legal; Accounting; A & R; Marketing and Sales; Promotion; Press, Publicity, and Advertising; Artist Relations; and Career Development.

Business Affairs Department. The Business Affairs Department, as its name implies, is charged with the responsibility of controlling the company's business direction. It's often staffed by attorneys, accountants, and other business-oriented persons. This department is historically a training ground for top label executives. Among other broad business-related duties, this department is responsible for negotiating and administering artists' contracts. Once a decision is made to sign an artist, the manager will be in contact with the Business Affairs Department. This department also usually has input into decisions involving tour support, promotion budgets, and the like. It's valuable for the manager to get to know the people in the Business Af-

fairs Department. Because of their background and responsibilities, they'll be much more likely to appreciate a
manager with a businesslike and professional approach to
his job. A favorable impression here never hurts.

Legal Department. The Legal Department at most companies is involved in drafting contracts, licenses, and other
legal documents negotiated by the Business Affairs Department. They're also called upon to render legal opinions
concerning various aspects of the label's operations.

Accounting Department. The Accounting Department
rounds out the business and financially oriented components of the company. The artist should have a special interest in this department because it's responsible for com-
puting and mailing him his royalty checks.

A & R Department. The A & R (Artist and Repertoire) Department is concerned with the artistic development of a
record company. As discussed earlier, the A & R Department is responsible for bringing new talent to the label. In
addition, it's their responsibility to serve as the creative
contact point between the artist, producer, and manager
and the company. They're involved in helping the artist
select material, studio, and producer. Often, the A & R man
acts as the production supervisor as well as artist's liaison
within the structure of the record company. Many A & R
men also fill a dual role of record producer. The A & R
Department will generally have input into any decision having to do with the creative matters affecting the label.

Marketing and Sales Department. The Marketing and
Sales Department is the lifeblood of the company. This
department is concerned with selling records that have
been developed through the efforts of the artist and the
A & R Department. It's very important that the marketing
specialists be excited about the artist's record. Without this
enthusiasm, it's difficult for them to convince distributors,
rack jobbers, and one stops of the saleability of the prod-

uct. A & R often will play a newly submitted tape by an unsigned artist or preliminary mixes on one of the label's current artists for the personnel in Marketing to get their opinion of the record's commercial viability. Once an artist is signed and a record completed, the Marketing and Sales staff will structure a marketing approach, along with the help of other departments such as A & R; Promotion; Press, Publicity and Advertising; Artist Relations; and Career Development. Once the record is released, this department makes sure product is available to retailers to fill the demand. It closely monitors sales and reports to other key departments at the label, as well as the manager. It's important for the manager to know the people in this department. An experienced manager can make a significant contribution to formulation of the marketing plan and can help the company make it work.

Promotion Department. Promotion goes hand in hand with Marketing and Sales. Once the record to be released is selected and the marketing approach is set, the Promotion Department will be involved in exposing that record in whatever manner the marketing plan dictates. This can mean getting AM and FM radio play, setting up promotion parties, in-store displays, and so forth. Most labels have field promotion men assigned to a specific territory. The home office coordinates their efforts on a daily basis and reports their progress in terms of airplay back to the department head, much in the same manner that Marketing tracks sales progress. The department head, in turn, analyzes and distributes this information to others in the company, as well as to the manager. This information is important in helping the label, manager, and artist know which move to make next.

Press, Publicity, and Advertising Department. Another key department to an effective marketing campaign, as well as to the artist's overall long-range career, is the Press, Publicity and Advertising Department. This component of the record company helps keep the artist's name before

the public either through press releases, trade and consumer stories, print ads, time buys, and other exposure
through the media. This is a tremendous asset available to
an artist. The manager can help assure that this tool is used
to its maximum effectiveness by constantly keeping the
department informed of every aspect of the artist's career
and by cooperating in arranging interviews, press conferences, and other publicity activities.

Artist Relations Department. The Artist Relations Department can be very helpful to the manager in areas of sched-
uling, routing, and attending to the numerous activities of a
busy artist. This department serves as a contact point between the artist and label. The manager should strive to
keep Artist Relations informed of the artist's schedule and
plans.

Career Development Department. Some of the larger
labels have a separate department devoted to the artist's
career development. This is a strong indication of the modern record company's commitment to the principle of
career longevity as opposed to a hit-and-miss approach
characterized by the one-shot hit record. Career Development acts much like an in-house manager, attending to
many management-oriented functions discussed in this
book. The record company feels this is necessary in many
cases in order to protect and develop their investment. This
is especially true in the case of young inexperienced artists
and unmanaged artists. An experienced and conscientious
manager can often accelerate the growth and development of his artist's career by working closely with this
department.

Coordination is obviously a problem in large department-
alized, multioffice record companies. Certain labels, such
as CBS, use product managers to help solve this problem.
The product manager is assigned to certain specified projects. It's his job to guide a particular artist's record through
every phase of the process we've just discussed. The manager obviously can be of great assistance to the product

manager in making the record a financial as well as an artistic success. Other labels may use the Career Development or A & R Department as the coordination and contact point for a specific artist or piece of product.

Working With the Record Company

With this basic outline of the record company's various functions and division of responsibility, let's now turn to some specific things the manager can do to help the record company help his artist.

Once the artist's recording contract has been negotiated with the Business Affairs Department, the manager should waste no time in meeting with the label executives to discuss the company's plans for the artist and his records. Most likely, this will have already been done prior to signing. An artist should never sign with a label until he has at least a basic understanding of the company's intentions. However, even assuming this phase has been completed, it's a good idea to reconfirm the previous discussions at the level of the president, if possible.

Next, the manager should spend whatever time necessary to meet everyone he possibly can who is connected with the label. This means going from department to department establishing one-to-one personal relationships with the various record company personnel. As pointed out in the chapter on the artist's development team, this does not mean department heads only. Everyone at the label, regardless of his particular responsibility, has a contribution to make to the artist's career. For this reason, the manager should take time to meet the individual promotion men, the press and publicity staff members, the secretaries, even the guy in the mailroom.

When he meets these people, he should tell them about the artist and his music, what he's trying to do, and where he's trying to go. He should make himself accessible, and ask for their thoughts and opinions.

After the manager has had a chance to get to know the record company personnel, he may want to introduce the artist to them. This has the tendency to reinforce the positive atmosphere the manager is trying to create.

In order for a record or an artist to achieve success with the public, those at the record company must first be excited and committed to the project or artist. These preliminary meetings are the first round in helping build that enthusiasm.

The business of selling records begins with the A & R Department. The manager should meet regularly with A & R to discuss the artist's material and production release schedule. Even though, by contract, the A & R Department may have final say as to material selection and release decisions, most often they'll take into consideration any recommendations and suggestions made by the manager, provided they're realistic and well thought out. The same is true of almost any other dealings with the record company. It's just human nature that a positive, cooperative approach to dealing with the artist's record company or any other development team member will result in more satisfactory results for the artist/client.

Once a collective decision has been made by the various departments within the company concerning what product will be released, the manager should turn his attention to the marketing scheme.

He should talk to the Marketing and Sales, Promotion and Press, Publicity and Advertising Departments about the artist's career-plan objectives and strategies. The emphasis here should be on arriving at a coordinated, unified approach, consistent with the artist's image and goals and the record company's assessment of how best to market the artist and his recordings. This should be a give-and-take discussion which hopefully will lead to a group consensus. This consensus will be the foundation of the marketing plan.

Prior to these discussions, the artist and manager should have carefully worked out their approach as to which route to take in maximizing the marketing and promotional efforts. Based on this, the manager is encouraged to work out general proposals in the areas of marketing, promotion, and press to present to the label. These general proposals should be flexible enough to conform to the views and circumstances of the record company. By making these proposals, the manager is at least assured of having some input into the final decision by the company. Even if his suggestions aren't adopted, he demonstrates his competency and ability to the label. Respect for the manager by the various department heads is extremely important to the manager's effectiveness.

When making proposals, it's very important for the manager to keep in mind that no one likes to be told how to do his job, though some people are more sensitive to this than others. The manager should always have an appreciation for the other person's psychological makeup and treat him accordingly. There's always the danger of the manager giving the appearance of taking over rather than merely giving suggestions. Conveying this impression should be avoided.

Once a marketing plan has been conceived, the manager's function becomes one of coordination. He must work with various label personnel and other members of the artist's development team to adequately prepare for the record's release. This will include coordinating with booking agents, promoters, publicity firms, television producers, and anyone else who will affect the record marketing process. If a tour is contemplated, tour support commitments must be finalized.

Once the record is released, the manager becomes the record company's point of contact with the artist. He should keep the various departments informed of the artist's schedule as well as any relevant developments pertaining to him. He should also make himself accessible to deal with any problem or new development that might arise.

The manager especially will want to maintain close contact with Marketing and Promotion concerning sales and airplay activity. Heavy sales or airplay in particular markets will affect decisions such as which dates to accept and which interviews should be granted.

If the artist is touring, arrangements must be made for press conferences, interviews, and in-store promotions.

This will necessitate coordination with the Artist Relations, Press, Publicity, and Advertising and Promotion Departments. The manager will want to review the crowd reaction to the artist's live performances with the Career Development Department and find out what impact the appearance is having on sales and airplay.

During the entire process, the manager and label must always be thinking about the artist's next recording session, next record release, and next tour. It's a never ending process requiring almost daily contact and communication with the various departments of the record company. However, it can be enormously rewarding if done effectively.

Summary
There's nothing more exciting for a manager than watching a record start to gain wide airplay and begin to break sales-wise, knowing that he's largely responsible for making it happen. This is a reward that can't be measured in terms of dollars and cents. It's the end result of months of planning, communication, and follow up with the record company. Major record companies have the resources and expertise available to achieve these results. It's up to the manager to insure that these assets are maximized in favor of the artist/client.

21.
The Road

The traveling and touring aspect of the artist's career is commonly referred to in the entertainment business as "the road" or "roadwork." To some entertainers, the road offers many exciting opportunities: the chance to meet new people, see new sights, and visit new cities or foreign countries. However, to other entertainers, the road is anything but exciting. These performers view it as a boring, monotonous existence that takes them away from family, home, and a normal way of life. Regardless of the artist's viewpoint, the road is an essential element in the careers of most artists.

Why Tour?
Touring has a direct and significant effect on an artist's popularity and audience appeal. The personal appearance is absolutely essential to the new artist trying to become known and develop a following. This is one of the few vehicles he has to display his talent and create a demand for himself and his art. This is especially true of new recording artists trying to establish record sales.

The road is equally important to the established artist from a career maintenance standpoint. To insure continued popularity, he must maintain visibility with his fans. Although television and records are devices available to him, there's no substitute for the personal appearance. This allows the audience to establish a closer relationship with him and serves as an effective means to add new fans to his following. With the competition for the entertainment dollar being so intense, no one in the industry today can afford to rest on his laurels or become aloof, forgetting the public. For those who do, there's the probability that the public will forget them and turn to other more active and visible artists.

Beyond developing and maintaining popularity, there's another very important reason why artists find the road a necessary part of their career—money. Concert, one-nighter, and club appearances account for a large portion of many artists' income. The fees earned from personal appearances can be substantial. Consequently, many artists can't afford to neglect the road from an income standpoint.

As mentioned earlier, a successful personal appearance tour is an excellent record promotion device that can translate into increased sales. Record companies frequently require that an artist be a working act before they'll sign a recording contract with him.

The road offers the artist the chance to impress thousands of people. A successful performance serves as reinforcement to existing fans and captures new followers. More people talking about the artist in a positive way attracts the curiosity of others. Good records, exciting performances, and positive feedback all translate into a popular artist. An impressive performance on stage or television fans the flames of popularity. Once the fire starts, the record company, booking agent, and manager need a balanced combination of dynamic live appearances and recordings to keep the fire spreading.

Since this aspect of the artist's career is so important, the manager must do everything possible to insure that his artist's live appearances are successful. Often a manager will travel with the artist, or be present at certain key engagements. When the manager is unable to travel with the artist, he usually employs a road manager. For all practical purposes, the road manager is an extension of the manager. He coordinates the numerous aspects of a personal appearance or tour, making hundreds of decisions daily.

Throughout the remaining portion of this chapter, we'll discuss the various functions of the manager and road manager relative to touring. While the following discussion assumes that the artist has chart activity at the time of the tour, these basic principles are still applicable in part to the artist without a record.

Preparing for the Tour

The manager's first order of business is setting an objective for each tour. (The word "tour" as used throughout this chapter refers not only to a series of dates but also to isolated engagements.) What is the artist trying to accomplish? Is the objective solely to enhance record sales? Is the goal perhaps to capture a specific market or region? Often the artist is trying to make as much money as possible within a particular time frame. The underlying objective will influence many of the manager's decisions when formulating the tour. Artist and manager must know exactly what they want the tour to achieve. Whatever the particular tour objective, it should be compatible with the artist's career goals.

Before accepting any dates, the manager must insure that the artist's act is ready for the road. He must work with the artist in developing a presentation not only pleasing to the artist but entertaining to the public. The stage show must be compatible with the artist's image. The live appearance must be tight and professionally produced. Ideally, an adequate amount of rehearsal time should be scheduled in order to allow the artist and manager to carefully develop and refine the act. During this time, decisions regarding material, arrangements, sequence, dramatic effects, lighting, sound, wardrobe, equipment, sidemen, choreography, background singers, and conductors should be made. Based on the objective of the tour and the artist's image, the presentation should be formulated, analyzed, and refined until both artist and manager are satisfied.

Once the artist and manager have made a decision regarding the format of the show, the on-stage support personnel, such as musicians and background vocalists, must be located and rehearsed. Simultaneously with rehearsal, the manager must employ off-stage support personnel, such as sound technicians, lighting crew, equipment handlers, drivers, and a road manager. All these decisions should be made within the guidelines of the tour's objective and image of the artist.

Also during the planning stage of the tour, the manager should meet with the artist's booking agent to discuss the objectives and structure of the tour and set a price range for the act. An experienced agent can provide valuable information concerning the marketability and price range of the artist based on the target markets, arena capacities, style of show, rider requirements, and current popularity of the artist. If the objectives of the artist are unrealistic, it's best to find out at this stage, before the support people are employed. Normally, a price range within which the booking agent can work is agreed upon by the agent and manager. Based on the asking price of the act, the manager will project the artist's overhead and costs associated with the production of the tour. If the general price limits are lower than previously estimated by the manager, modifications may have to be implemented to reduce the cost of producing the show.

Assuming that the booking agent is confident the price for the artist can be attained without difficulty, the next consideration is the availability of the artist. This will depend on the existing schedule of the artist and the length and type of engagements the artist seeks to undertake.

Once the manager and booking agent have thoroughly discussed and reviewed the scope of the artist's tour, the manager will need to know how long it will take to set the tour. Here's where an artist's popularity pays dividends. If the artist has a hot record on the charts, coupled with a reputation for first-class personal appearances, the agent should be able to set the tour easily, provided that the price is not out of line. It should be noted that, with a superstar, price is usually a lesser consideration because the talent buyer knows that the concert will most likely be an automatic sellout. Conversely, if the artist doesn't have a current record release and isn't known for his ability as a performer, the agent's job will be much more difficult.

Artists often become upset if the booking agent can't deliver the type of dates for the desired amount of money. Although booking agents do have some influence on the marketing process of the artist, they don't control every aspect. They must work with the product as it exists. Once the artist has expended the resources available to him through artist's development team members, such as his record company, public relations firm, booking agent, and manager, the decision to book the artist is up to the buyer. His decision is based upon his perception of the commercial potential of the artist to sell concert tickets. That perception is based on the artist's past personal appearances, overall reputation, and current record-chart activity. The agent can give his best effort and still not achieve the desired results for the artist because many of the factors influencing the buyer's decision are beyond the booking agent's control. Of course, in some instances, the agent may be the deciding factor that influences the customer's decision. Therefore, it's important that the manager maintain a close working relationship with the booking agent since his confidence, belief, and excitement about the artist can definitely influence customers' buying habits. However, it would be unrealistic to think that the booking agent can control the talent buyer's decisionmaking process. The act must be able to stand on its own merits.

The Artist Relations; Marketing; Press, Publicity, and Advertising; and Promotion Departments of the artist's record company should also be advised of the tour arrangements. In order to achieve maximum benefit, the various departments of the record company will require a certain amount of lead time to activate their promotional machinery. For the artist, booking agent, and record company to achieve maximum benefit, they must all move in a carefully coordinated manner. A successful tour depends on the interplay of these members of the artist's development team. The record company, therefore, should also have input in setting tour objectives and target areas. This is especially true when the record company is providing the artist with tour support money.

As the booking agent receives offers from buyers, they're communicated to the manager, who may accept or reject them at his discretion. If the offer is in a desired market and within the price range previously established with the booking agent, the manager will probably accept it. However, supporting dates, routing, travel factors, and overall tour developments could force a negative decision. If the offer is beyond the designated market area or the price is under the minimum agreed on, it will probably be rejected. However, the financial or promotional value of a supporting date, in some instances, will force the manager to depart from the original tour plan. Submitting each offer to the manager affords him the opportunity to follow the development of the tour. Depending upon the circumstances, he then may approve a price or change of direction if he feels it's necessary.

As each date is booked, the agent will usually send a press kit to the employer containing the artist's latest record, photographs, biography, and other promotional material. Often the artist's public relations firm, record company, and manager will send additional promotional material to insure that the employer receives adequate publicity. The booking agent will issue performance contracts to the employer. The booking agent will also forward a signed copy of each contract to the local office of the American Federation of Musicians or other applicable labor organization in the city where the engagement will take place.

While the booking agent and record company prepare for the upcoming dates, the manager will be busy finalizing the tour personnel, acquiring needed equipment, and making transportation arrangements. A road manager must be employed if one is not already on staff. Normally, most touring artists have a full-time road manager. In all the tour preparations yet to be discussed, the road manager will work very closely with the manager.

The next phase of tour preparation involves three important areas: travel, public relations, and protective functions.

Travel Arrangements. After the tour dates have been set, the road manager will usually make the hotel and travel arrangements. Moreover, arrangements will have to be made for ground transportation if the artist or support team plans to travel by air. Otherwise, the road manager should inspect the vehicles that will be used to be certain that they're safe, comfortable, and efficient. Here, we're referring to buses, automobiles, and equipment trucks. A travel agent is often used to make hotel and travel arrangements. When this is done, the road manager acts as liaison between the travel agent and artist's tour personnel. The road manager must also make sure that all members of the tour have valid passports when traveling abroad, and that they're affiliated with the necessary labor organizations. While many travel arrangements can be made in advance of the tour, there will always be problems or changes in schedule which will necessitate the road manager making modifications in advance plans.

Public Relations. The public relations function of the road manager is often overlooked due to more pressing duties associated with the tour. Public relations awareness on the part of the road manager can prove to be a real asset to the overall career development of the artist. A substantial part of the road manager's public relations work can be done before the tour begins. The names and addresses of key radio stations, program directors, and disc jockeys; television stations and newspapers; music equipment stores; local union representatives; as well as record stores, promotion men, and distributors in the cities the artist will be performing should be assembled in directory form. The road manager should make an effort to develop a friendly relationship with all these people by contacting them in advance of the engagements. It's also a good idea to invite these people to the artist's engagement and to send them press kits. As a follow up to this initial contact, the record company should be instructed to send complimentary records and other information about the artist. In addition, the record company should be kept current on all tour developments. An itinerary of the artist's tour, including the exact date, place, and time of each engagement, should be sent to key record-company personnel. This information will allow the record company to stay current with the artist's tour to insure that the record product is in the stores and that promotional efforts are being coordinated. As stated previously, many record companies help the artist financially via tour support monies or promotional campaigns for artist's records prior to the engagement. The manager and road manager must keep the record companies up to date in order for the promotion to achieve optimum results.

The road manager should also contact the employer (or promoter) to insure that he's received adequate publicity material. At this time, any questions regarding the artist's rider requirements, location of engagement, or other matters relative to the performance can be discussed. Again, we must stress the importance of the road manager establishing a personal relationship with the employer prior to the arrival of the artist. Once the road manager arrives in a tour date city, he should attempt to personally meet all the people with whom he has previously communicated. If this is impossible, and it often is, he should try to call and invite them to the artist's performance.

Protective Functions. The last general area of a road manager's duties involves precautionary measures to insure the successful completion of the tour. The first preventative step is for the road manager to know where to reach the manager at all times during the tour. This is absolutely imperative. The road manager should have in his possession photostatic copies of the artist performance contracts, including all riders and special attachments. If a problem occurs with an employer, it's best that the road manager have a copy of the contract rather than just a route sheet with engagement information.

The road manager should maintain an important papers file containing names, addresses, telephone and social security numbers, local affiliation, passports, and emergency contacts for all members in the tour. All vehicle ownership and registration documents should also be included in this file. If the artist's personnel are covered under a hospitalization insurance policy, the necessary identification forms should be on file. If each member maintains his own medical insurance coverage, the road manager should have a photocopy of the policy and identification card. A duplicate set of the entire file should be kept at the manager's office in the event the road manager's file is lost or destroyed.

Advance plans should be made with the manager or artist's accountant regarding the bookkeeping procedure to be utilized during the tour. The road manager should fully understand the procedure and have an ample supply of accounting forms. In addition, he should have at least two major credit cards and an adequate amount of cash. However, carrying large sums of money on the road should be avoided. If possible, all payments from employers for artist's services should be in the form of cashiers or certified checks. When the road manager does receive cash, interbank deposits should be used to transfer the money quickly, thus avoiding accumulation of substantial amounts of cash.

Contacting the local musicians' union representative in advance of the tour can be helpful if it's necessary for the road manager to replace a musician for an engagement due to accident, sickness, or other unforeseen emergency. When personnel problems arise during a tour, the road manager must act decisively. Substantial income could be lost unless the problem is solved quickly. The local union representative is a good starting point, especially if the road manager is on a first name basis with him.

If the artist will be traveling by automobile or the equipment will be transported by truck, it's wise for the road manager to know in advance the names of local dealerships representing the brand vehicle being used. A telephone call and an autographed picture to a dealer in the city in which the artist is performing not only helps if extraordinary service is needed, but may even create another fan for the artist. Another precautionary measure regarding ground transportation is to maintain a good relationship with a major rental car company. Again, a personal relationship, or simply knowing who to contact at three in the morning, can help tremendously when the group needs a vehicle to make it to the next date.

On the Road

Once the tour has begun, the road manager's responsibilities increase and the amount of time to make decisions decreases. His primary function is to insure the artist's timely arrival at the place of the engagement. Whether traveling by air, car, or bus, the problem of coordinating departure, arrival, and alternate modes of transportation in the event of schedule changes is ever-present.

Assuming artist and support crew arrive without any problem, the road manager should focus his concern on the stage setup. Through advance communication with the employer, the road manager can arrange for the arena to be open for the road crew at the desired time. An efficient road crew is not only advantageous to the artist, but also economically helpful to a promoter when union stagehands are being paid on an hourly rate.

Following a trouble-free stage setup, the road manager should supervise the sound check and brief rehearsal, if desired by the artist. The arena should be closed to the public during this phase of activity. Once the road manager leaves the arena, security people should be present until the equipment is dismantled.

While the stage is being set up, the road manager should inspect the dressing rooms to insure that they're adequate, and he should determine their proximity to the artist's entrance and exit into the arena. If the artist requires food and beverage in the dressing room, this should be arranged.

The road manager should attempt to structure the artist's daily schedule to allow sufficient time for rest prior to each performance. While this can be an extremely difficult task, he must make every effort to insure that the artist is well rested before each performance.

On the night of the show, the road manager is responsible for all last-minute details. He must see that the artist's show begins on time and runs smoothly. The road manager acts as a field general for the lights, stage crew, sound man, and all other support personnel. Depending on the type of engagement, it may be necessary for him to review the ticket manifest and receipts to determine if percentage fees have been earned and properly paid.

The road manager should evaluate all aspects of the artist's show. Was the performance too long? Was audience reaction enthusiastic? Did the lighting effects dramatize the performance? A written report of each performance should be forwarded to the manager immediately after each engagement. These reports serve as a diary of the tour. They also serve as a directory of all the people involved in the production of each show. After the tour is completed, these people should be contacted by telephone or letter thanking them for their help. Once an engagement has been successfully completed, the road manager should turn his attention to the next date, and so on, until the tour is concluded.

We've attempted to discuss the many functions of a road manager during an extended tour; however, to cover them all is impossible. Whatever problem may occur, it's the road manager's duty to deal with it, while insulating the artist from as much unnecessary distraction during the tour as possible.

After the Tour

The manager must make the final determination of the success of the tour. The reports filed by the road manager serve not only as a good control device, but also as a reference in evaluating the tour's results. The record company can provide the manager with sales figures of the artist's product after the tour. This is a good way to measure the degree of the artist's impact on a particular market after the concert. The booking agent will be directly in contact with the employer or promoter after the event. Here, too, is a reliable source of feedback concerning the artist's performance.

After the tour is completed, the total picture can be analyzed. At best, the manager hopes to find universal acceptance in all markets where the artist performed. He's not interested in scattered success in pushover markets. The artist and manager shouldn't be satisfied with a tour that elicits mixed reactions or audience indifference.

Summary
The road is probably the most demanding and challenging aspect of the artist's career. In many ways, it's also the most important and satisfying. As with every other area of the artist's career, planning, hard work, and follow-through add up to success.

22.
Re-evaluation and Critique

It's extremely difficult for a highly successful artist to remain objective about his career. However, to insure that success continues, he must always be open to re-evaluation and critique from his manager. While the large royalty checks, lucrative performance contracts, and thunderous applause are all evidence that the artist has made it, someone must retain a realistic perspective. The same goes for a new artist who begins to experience success. In both situations, this responsibility falls to the manager.

Some artists find criticism distasteful and deflating to their egos. Their positive self-image is reinforced by the acclaim heaped upon them by the public and press. "If I'm so wrong, why are my concerts still packed and record sales soaring?" they retort. Unfortunately, an artist who can't accept any constructive critique of his career has lost all perspective—the life expectancy of his career will be short. On the other hand, the mature professional will acknowledge the common bond between him and the sources of meaningful criticism. It's only common sense that the artist's manager, record company, producer, and booking agent all want the artist's career to flourish and sustain itself for as long as possible. When the artist succeeds, they succeed. The advice that they give, therefore, is motivated by a common economic bond between them and the artist. The astute artist will realize this and listen openly to a constructive analysis of his work.

Re-evaluating the Artist and His Act

The manager should review all facets of the artist's stage personality. Does he have bad stage habits? Has the artist become complacent? Is the artist overexposed or underexposed? What has audience reaction been to the artist's live performance? All areas of the artist's act need review and scrutiny.

Once the manager has presented his assessment of the positive and negative points of the artist's work, both should discuss ways to improve the weak areas without sacrificing the strong points. While the artist and manager always make the final decision on matters affecting the artist's career, their willingness to consider the opinions of others can often help keep their perspective clear.

At this point, any artist who has retained a "yes man" for a manager is probably going to be in trouble. It's unlikely that a manager who can only maintain his job by constantly agreeing with the artist can offer any constructive comments if they conflict with the artist's viewpoint. So instead of having an advisor, the artist has retained another follower—something he could get for much less than the percentage he pays him.

The business structure and operation of the artist should also be re-evaluated periodically during each year. All legal documents should be reviewed, insurance coverages updated if necessary, and accounting records audited. The artist's budget should be carefully studied to determine if any breakdowns or excesses have occurred during the year. Often, the annual summary reflects the accumulation of various expenses that have previously gone unnoticed but prove to be significant at year's end. Once detected, adjustments for such expenditures can be made in the new budget. All reports to governmental authorities relative to the artist's business should be prepared, explained to the artist, and filed with the proper authority. Since many of the business aspects of an artist's career won't be understood by him, the manager would be well advised to request a letter from the accountant, attorney, and insurance agent reviewing their particular area of the artist's business for the year. The manager can then wrap up the review of the artist's business operation at a meeting specifically for that purpose. If the artist has questions or desires additional information, the manager can offer the summary letters to help clarify his business status. In some instances, it may be best if the accountant, attorney, and other advisors are present at the annual business meeting to personally answer any inquires from the artist. Regardless of procedure, at least one meeting a year should be devoted to an evaluation and review of all aspects of the artist's business.

The creative evaluation cannot be forced into a predetermined time frame as easily as the business review. Since styles and trends in the entertainment industry change so rapidly, this area must be constantly under managerial scrutiny. The guiding principle for the artist and manager in this area is the artist's image. All factors affecting image must be coordinated to enhance rather than distort the artist's image. If, however, a major change in image is desired, then the artist and manager should consult all members of the development team before embarking on such a far-reaching move. A total departure from an established image could result in professional suicide for the artist.

Projecting and Enhancing the Artist's Image

Let's assume that the artist and manager are satisfied with the artist's current image. Their primary concern, then, is the proper maintenance of that image. Several factors must be reviewed in assessing the efficiency of team members in projecting and enhancing the artist's image.

The Artist's Material. The first important factor is the selection of artist's material for recording and live performances. Where is the material coming from—the artist or other songwriters? The material must be compatible with the artist's voice, style, and abilities. Usually the artist that composes his own material has a common thread running through most of his compositions. The artist that must rely on music publishers and songwriters must be careful not to select material totally inconsistent with his image.

The Record Producer. Another key influence affecting artist's image that should be evaluated periodically is the record producer. The artist and manager must review the producer's work product in view of the artist's goals, not the producer's. For instance, let's suppose an artist and producer have been working together for several years, finally achieving some degree of success on the last album they recorded. The record company wants the followup album to be in the same vein in order to enhance the artist's image and take advantage of the record-buying following created by the last album release. However, the success of the previous album has afforded the producer a new-found degree of financial security. Despite the commercial success of the record, he's not pleased with the overall sound of the artist's material and demands a radical change in direction. What should the artist do? He believes in the producer's ability as a result of the success of the last album. But the artist also believes in the recording direction suggested by the record company. The manager must resolve the dilemma without compromising the direction and image of the artist. If the producer is diverting the artist from his strategical course, then a new producer may be in order. The manager can't let the producer satisfy his artistic aspirations at the expense of his artist. To guard against this situation, the artist-producer relationship should be examined at certain intervals.

The Record Company. The effectiveness of the record company should also be assessed at various stages, depending upon the terms of the recording contract. The manager must be aware of personnel and organizational changes occurring within the record company that could be detrimental to the artist. The resignation or retirement of key record-company executives, mergers, acquisitions, and shifts in company policies—all could have some affect on the artist's relationship with the record company.

The following illustration is a practical application of this potential problem. You'll recall Paul Chaffey and London Smile from an earlier chapter. After signing with the record company, they developed a close relationship with the A & R man responsible for their record contract. Throughout their relationship, that A & R man promoted London Smile within the company structure. Since the group was achieving steady record sales, both record company and artist were pleased with the relationship. In the years to come, the friendly A & R man was promoted up the corporate ladder and eventually was hired as president of a competing record company. Since he left, the company doesn't seem to be as enthusiastic about the group as it once was. London Smile's contract will soon be up for renewal at the option of both parties. The group's friend wants London Smile to sign with his company. Interesting situation.

The purpose of this hypothetical story is to illustrate the vulnerability of the artist to change in the organization as well as the industry environment. The future of London Smile could be affected, given the injection of various circumstances. Is the company their friend now leads a stable one? Has the relationship with the existing company been good? What will each company offer the group? Is the existing record company getting ready to go through organizational changes that could be detrimental to the group? The answer to any one of these questions could affect Paul Chaffey's decision as to which company he should recommend to his clients. This points up the importance of keeping attuned to the inner workings of the record company.

The Booking Agent. The artist and booking agent relationship also requires periodic evaluation. Here again, the artist may become affiliated with a certain agency because of a particular individual. The artist may be affected if that individual leaves the agency or is transferred into another area of the agency's operation. This is always a consideration in reviewing the artist's agency relationship.

As mentioned in a previous chapter, many booking agencies specialize in specific types of performances or are confined to certain geographic regions. While one agency may be ideal for an artist at an early stage of his career, a shift in direction or a new level of career success may render the agency incapable of helping the artist.

For instance, let's assume that an artist has been performing quite successfully in the club market for a number of years. While interested in recording, the artist has never stressed this aspect of his career, since his club dates provide him with a substantial income. Although not recording frequently, the recordings submitted to various record companies are impressive. The artist is eventually signed by a major label and, within six months, an album and single are released. The response is overwhelming—both the single and album soar up the charts. The record company, astonished with this new-found success, releases another single and it too climbs the charts. Eagerly, the record company encourages the artist to set a tour to capitalize on the market acceptance. But the booking agency that was so successful in securing the artist club engagements isn't capable of arranging the concert dates. As a result, the agency attempts to keep the artist in club markets. Asked for a partial release so the artist can retain another agent for concert dates, the agency reacts negatively.

Here, again, a change in the artist's career dictates a different type of input from the agency member of his development team. Such situations are not uncommon in the entertainment business. The manager must scrutinize the booking-agent relationship to insure that this aspect of the artist's business is deriving maximum economic benefit.

Other Image-Related Components. All other components of the artist's image must be inspected to complete the re-evaluation process. The critique should apply to the sound and lighting crews, music director, sidemen, and all other personnel utilized by the artist. The public relations firm and road manager should also come under the magnifying glass. Their activities are vital to the proper maintenance and projection of the artist's image.

Artist/Management Relationship. The artist and manager should also evaluate their own relationship as objectively as possible. Has the relationship been successful? Has this manager been good for the artist's career? Are both moving toward the accomplishment of predetermined career goals? After an objective analysis, both parties may agree that a termination of the relationship is best for artist and manager. If either party disagrees about prematurely ending the relationship, then their differences should be compromised or attempts made to settle them. If this can't be done, both parties must consider a release as a possible solution to their problem. If so, then this should be conducted as professionally and honorably as possible.

Career Goals and Strategies. The artist's career goals and strategies should also be reviewed periodically in order to utilize them effectively. The artist may wish to change career direction, or maybe set new goals. Whatever the case, a periodic re-evaluation will insure that career goals, strategies, and tactics will be kept current.

Summary
The manager should attempt to give the artist an overview of his entire operation, a concise review of the business machinery, and an in-depth discussion of all the creative factors influencing the artist's image. Critical comments from the artist's development team members also should be considered and discussed. All phases of the artist's career should be reviewed, from the selection of material for recording, to the color of his shoes on stage. The manager should recap the year in terms of success in achieving desired goals, and discuss the modification or selection of new goals. As previously stated, career strategies and tactics should be scrutinized and altered if necessary. During the re-evaluation, the manager shouldn't hesitate to discuss the artist's failures as well as his successes during the year. The artist must discipline himself to use valid criticism to maintain and accelerate his career development.

Part V
Mastering Success

23.
Coping With Fame

Louie Richards' career was a success story. At the age of thirteen, Louie was playing in local rock 'n roll bands. By the time he was seventeen, he was a veteran performer, experienced in recording. For the next twelve years, no one was more devoted to achieving success in the entertainment business than Louie. But throughout his career he encountered numerous personnel changes within his group, financial hardship, and untold personal problems.

Although Louie had married young, fortunately he had an extremely understanding wife who encouraged him to pursue his music career. She worked to support them throughout his career. Time and time again her income pulled them through the hard times.

Since the beginning of his career, Louie had recorded literally hundreds of tracks. He had the experience, talent, determination, and dedication to be a success in the entertainment business. Yet, after sixteen years as a professional artist, he still hadn't experienced a chart record. All his friends and fellow musicians agreed that Louie had "paid dues" long enough.

Then, at age twenty-nine, all the experience paid off in success beyond Louie's wildest dreams. Within a year, his recordings were being hailed as the most progressive sounds of the decade. To the general public Louie was an overnight success. Only his wife and friends knew the truth.

This sudden success brought all the fame and recognition Louie could have ever wanted. And with fame came money. In less than two years after his career had begun to take off, Louie had earned ten times the money that he had in all of his previous years as an entertainer. Louie could do nothing wrong; everything he did was deemed sensational.

After the initial shock of success had passed, people close to Louie noticed a change in his personality and attitude. He was far less friendly and down-to-earth. At times, he acted like a spoiled kid.

Louie and his wife also started experiencing real domestic problems for the first time in their marriage. Louie's new-found wealth made it possible for his wife to accompany him on the road during tours. During the years Louie was struggling, he and his wife dreamed of the day they both could be together to enjoy the excitement of travel and meeting new people. However, now that the opportunity existed, it was nothing like they'd expected. The more time they spent together, the more arguments resulted. Louie grew tired of having her around. On the road, he was a star, and she didn't fit into his lifestyle. As far as Louie was concerned, they were in different worlds. Unfortunately, the inevitable occurred. Louie and his wife were divorced.

Louie was so wrapped up in being a star that his divorce didn't really bother him at the time. His immediate concern was his health. The hectic schedule was causing him minor sickness and ailments much too often. Louie seemed tired all the time. He just didn't seem to have time to exercise or care for himself. Things were moving too fast. Though he knew his diet was poor and schedule too hectic, Louie was still having the best time of his life.

Besides being in poor physical shape and attempting to maintain the fast pace of his schedule, Louie also started drinking much too often. While the alcohol had a stimulating effect, enabling Louie to maintain his rigorous schedule, his physical well-being and mental outlook deteriorated quickly. Time and time again, his manager begged him to slow down. But Louie was making so much money, that he simply buried his problems with cars, new homes, beautiful women, parties, and more alcohol. Since all these things seemed to cure his emotional and physical depressions, he repeatedly returned to them for comfort. Louie's prescription for his depression was money. He had plenty of it, and as long as it was coming in he could afford the expensive pain-killers.

Three years after Louie had acquired the Midas touch, it slowly started to fade. His manager was the first to recognize the situation. He'd been with Louie from the very beginning and knew him better than anyone else. They'd always gotten along marvelously and had the utmost respect for each other. Sensing a shift in musical styles, Louie's manager recommended that he reduce his live appearances and devote a substantial amount of his time to recording. While this would reduce his current income, his manager believed it would help Louie physically as well as professionally. Louie panicked. The thought of slowing down, even the least bit, was totally foreign to him. Along with the fear of losing his fans, money, and expensive pleasures, Louie's warped perspective of life added to the dilemma.

His solution was simple. "Book me more dates for more money." When his manager attempted to explain the harm in such action, Louie exploded. "Everybody who is making money off me will do what I say or else." The decision was final. Louie would call the shots with or without his manager or anybody else, if necessary. Unfortunately for Louie, he communicated his career philosophy to his agent and record company in the same obnoxious tone.

As his career continued to gradually slow down, the economic consequences started showing up in smaller record royalty checks and less money for live performances. To make matters worse, Louie didn't really care about his performances. All he was interested in was the money. His gratification didn't come from the applause of the audience or from shouts for encores, but only from dollars. Although his income was still substantial by anyone's standards, it wasn't enough to sustain the lifestyle he'd cultivated. His manager attempted to regulate his personal finances by continually warning him he was spending money that should be invested or set aside for income tax payments. All to no avail. Louie became fed up with his manager's overprotective attitude and continual advice. He simply tuned him out entirely. Finally, his manager, realizing he could do nothing for Louie, reluctantly and sadly resigned.

The scenerio continued for less than a year, until Louie's drinking problem became so bad that it dominated his entire life. This, in turn, accelerated the decline of his career. Four years after Louie's dream had come true, it had ended. Now, without his wife's comfort and his manager's advice, what was he going to do? Yes, Louie Richards' career was a success—or was it?

Again, we've used a hypothetical example to portray how elusive success can be. Contained in this scenerio were many "success crisis" signals that may be helpful to artist and manager attempting to avoid this trap. Unfortunately, the story of Louie Richards is repeated all too frequently in the entertainment industry. The true stories have different facts or distinguishing twists, but the ending is basically the same. These stories all pose the same question: How do artist and manager cope with fame?

Avoiding a Success Crisis

One of the primary factors causing a success crisis is the sudden accumulation of substantial amounts of income earned by an artist in a short period of time. The development process of most artists takes many years. As with Louie Richards, artists receive relatively little compensation during this "dues-paying" period. It is a time of sacrifice, usually without financial reward. But, when success does come, the reverse is true. Almost overnight, artists can be making more money than they can spend. This gives a false impression of the future because the money being earned at the height of the artist's career won't continue forever. The initial shock of increased earnings must be handled cautiously by artist and manager. Much attention should be devoted to the financial-planning aspect of the artist's career at the first sign of such a situation.

We contend that the earnings for many successful artists tend to follow a pattern. That is, low income during the development phase, followed by a substantial jump once success is achieved, which will rise to its highest point, followed by a gradual decline to a point higher than where the artist began but lower than the peak point of earnings. The objective of the manager is to achieve the highest income point for the artist and then sustain it as long as possible. The artist's income cycle often will peak and fall several times during his career. His starting income position will be higher or lower depending on the particular artist. Nonetheless, we believe a basic pattern exists, and at some point the artist will experience a concentrated income over a brief timespan. Therefore, it's certainly understandable why an artist could lose perspective of financial reality. After starving and sacrificing for a long period of time and then almost in a flash start receiving checks for $5,000, $10,000, and $50,000 from record companies, publishers, and concert buyers—yes, that would tend to distort anyone's view of the future.

The manager should be aware of this trap and have a general idea of what he'd do in the event such a situation occurs. Although some may label such a plan as daydreaming, it could well become a reality in the fast-changing entertainment business.

Warning Signals

Success in large doses can often bring about physical abuses. Having enough money to buy anything he wants can be a disaster if the artist isn't prepared for it. Without a proper handle on life, the money earned by a successful artist could afford him access to alcohol, drugs, sex, and material possessions in excessive quantities. Take Louie Richards, for example. His money gave him the opportunity to obtain alcohol in any quantity he desired. All people face this potential danger, but few have the economic capacity to truly indulge. The manager must caution his artist to

avoid a "materialistic rampage." This can be a very delicate area, but the manager must speak out if his artist's
health or financial well being is threatened, even if the artist
himself is the adversary. In situations where the artist refuses to take counsel and continues on a destructive
course, the manager must exercise extreme caution. If advice and persuasion fail, the manager should best leave a
trail of paper to support his objections to the artist's damaging activity. When the inevitable crash does occur, an artist
might start looking for a scapegoat. This is especially true
of artists whose egos are out of control. Not being able to
accept the fact their actions led to their own downfall,
they're forced to find a guilty party to protect their infallible
self-image.

Some situations may become so unbearable that the artist not only refuses to take the manager's advice, but
begins to hold the manager in contempt as being an incompetent. For the experienced manager, this situation
has only one solution—termination of his relationship with
the artist. While the economic consequences can be pain-
ful, the manager must think about his future. If an artist has
gotten totally out of control, cancelling engagements, refus-
ing to record, and taking his public for granted, his career
will eventually fall apart regardless of his past successes.
Since this type of conduct reflects directly on the manager's reputation, then after all has been done to salvage
the artist's career, it's best to let the artist suffer the consequences of his own decisions.

Another warning signal of a pending success crisis is
complacency or laziness. The artist could be handling the
emotional and financial aspects of a successful career, but
fall into a far different trap. It's the "I've made it" attitude.
In the entertainment business, an artist is only as successful as his accomplishments today. Yesterday doesn't
count. One of the characteristics of entertainment is ever-
changing styles that lead to frequent star turnover. Unless
the artist is ready for retirement, he must be prepared to
work just as hard once success is achieved as he did
earlier. The big difference in the case of the successful art-

ist is that the monetary rewards and recognition are far more extensive in the successful phase than they were in the development phase.

Summary

All too often an artist will have a hit record and believe there's no tomorrow or end to the success. But this is a fallacy. You need only look at the current record charts to confirm this fact. How many new artists are included on the Hot 100 now who weren't there a year ago? By the same token, the number of veteran artists who have sustained their careers also is evidence that an artist can overcome changes in styles and fads, and can retain and enhance his popularity and appeal.

The artist who obtains a high level of success in the entertainment industry is well advised to be constantly aware of how to deal with the many dangers we've discussed. No matter what happens to any particular artist, the entertainment business will continue, with or without him. Over the years, the industry has lost gigantic superstars because of death or self-imposed retirement, yet, there's always been someone to fill the vacancy they've left. No one is that important or that necessary.

The financial rewards of a successful career, if handled properly, can provide lifelong compensation for a job well done. The accolades of the public can help the artist achieve the total self-fulfillment that few people ever have the opportunity to experience. Effective management, a realistic approach to fame and fortune, and common sense are the qualities every artist needs to master success.

24.
Money Management

What exactly is money? "Money" is generally defined as "anything that serves as a common measure of value, or as a means for the payment of debts or services rendered." "Save your money, spend it sparingly and wisely, work hard, and get to bed early," said Poor Richard. Money motivates all of us to some degree. The accumulation of money affords us the opportunity to fulfill our needs, both physically and psychologically. But can we really ever have enough money to buy or obtain everything we may want in a lifetime? No! It's all relative to the earnings of an individual. The up-and-coming, starving artist wishes he had enough money to pay his car note and guitar payment. The moderately successful artist is plagued with paying for a home, sports car, and a more expensive guitar. The star who's earning plenty of money still has problems. By the time Uncle Sam takes his chunk, there's barely enough money left to make the payments on his three homes, four cars, and nothing left for that sixteenth guitar he must have. No matter how much an artist makes, there'll never be enough money for everything.

There's an art to making money. The purpose of this book is to help artist and manager obtain success, which in itself will gain each economic rewards—money. But that's just half the problem. Once the artist has acquired money, he must try to keep it. The preservation of money requires just as much talent, if not more, than acquiring it. The objective of this chapter is to survey the various areas that will require attention if the artist is to preserve the rewards of his labor.

As previously stated, the artist must first make money in order to become a candidate for the second problem, that is, preserving it. While we will discuss this problem in terms of the successful artist, the manager is also advised to consider these principles in order to maintain his own financial position.

Furthermore, the manager also should be generally aware of these financial considerations so that he can serve his client to the fullest extent. This is not to say that the manager should attempt to be an accountant, tax planner, investment counselor, and so on. But an awareness of these money management areas will make it possible for the manager to know when to solicit professional expertise in these diverse and complex matters.

The money management areas can be divided into five parts. They are: Income/Expense Control; Investments: Tax Planning; Retirement; and Estate Planning.

Income/Expense Control

The Budget. In an earlier chapter we discussed the importance of a budget. A well-thought-out budget is the first step to financial planning. It serves as a roadmap to one's financial future. Assuming expense and income budgets have been carefully prepared, several financial control devices should be implemented. An accounting system must be set up on a weekly, monthly, or per engagement basis to accurately record the income and expense flow of the artist. Many artists have unique accounting systems prepared by their managers or accountants to fill this need. These "roadsheets" are the first line of financial record-keeping and are essential to maintaining an accurate financial picture of the artist's expenses.

Profit-and-Loss Statement and Balance Sheet. At the end of each accounting period (monthly, quarterly, semi-annually, or annually) the accountant should prepare a profit-and-loss statement and balance sheet. As stated earlier, the budget is analogous to a traveler viewing a road map before a trip. The profit-and-loss statement is the traveler's log of what has happened during the trip and a description of the exact route taken. The balance sheet is a picture of the artist's economic condition, assets, and liabilities at a given time—it's comparable to a photograph of the trip at a certain point. These three financial tools will provide the artist and manager with the basic information needed to maintain control over operating incomes and expenses. Of course, as the artist becomes more successful and his income increases, the accountant may want to implement additional accounting procedures to keep a closer watch over the artist's financial well being.

The manager's awareness of the artist's sources of income and expenses becomes an extremely valuable tool when modifications have to be made in revenue inflows or outflows. For example, if the artist's popularity starts to fade, causing his engagement price to fall, the manager may want to implement cost-reduction procedures to insulate the artist from personnal loss of income. Conversely, if the artist is making too much money, the manager may recommend increasing some expenses to help reduce net profit in order to put the artist in a lower tax bracket.

The same accounting procedures should be followed for the artist's personal earnings. Once the booking agent, manager, support crew, attorneys, public relations firm, travel costs and other expenses have been paid, the artist will receive the balance. The amounts of money earned by the artist should be controlled just as carefully as the business earnings. The artist should maintain a personal budget, profit-and-loss statement, and balance sheet. Again, it makes spotting unnecessary economic drains much easier and helps the artist to be aware of where all his money is going. Remember, no matter how much an artist makes, there's never enough for everything. The successful artist will have to establish some priorities as to his needs and desires. Once this is done, his cash outflow can follow a logical pattern instead of resembling an irrational spending spree.

Credit. Another important aspect of income-expense control is the proper utilization of credit. Used wisely, credit is a most valuable ally; however, uncontrolled credit can result in the utter destruction of the user. Even the improper use of the most common credit outlets can result in harsh consequences.

A hypothetical story will help to illustrate this point. A young group of artists had just made the transition from "weekend warriors" to full-time professional entertainers. Faced with considerable travel commitments, the group leader procured credit cards from every major oil company. The cards were used indiscriminately, depending on which dealer was the most convenient at the time fuel was needed. When the monthly statements arrived, it was easy to let them slide in lieu of more pressing expenses, such as salaries, motel bills, and equipment payments, since no one gas bill was that large. The following month the same procedure was repeated. After eight months, even though small payments had been made, the group realized they had a major bill confronting them. The group had been partially financing itself by using its gas credit cards. After a short period of time, the gas companies started revoking their cards and began instigating legal proceedings to collect the amounts due. This situation made it exceedingly difficult to get a bank loan to pay the accumulated debt.

Credit card debt is fine for short-run financial help, but it's not a permanent or long-run solution. The artists could have avoided this embarrassing situation by seeking financial help from their banker in the beginning instead of waiting till their credit was nearly destroyed. Beware of credit-card debt. The artist can use the card for short-run expenses, but should make plans to pay the debt during the accounting time period it is incurred. By doing this, he won't develop a false sense of financial well being.

The artist must also be cautious about the use of long-term bank debt or mortgage debt, both from a business and personal standpoint. The advice of an accountant, business advisor, or manager well versed in business practices can be extremely useful in restraining the artist from overloading his debt position.

For the young artist, usually the reverse is true. He can't get enough financing to help develop his act due to the risky nature of the business. Here, too, the advice of a professional can be useful in helping the artist acquire the financing necessary to develop his career. In today's society, debt is almost a necessity. Used wisely, it can be the catalyst in making fortunes. Used improperly, it can lead to bankruptcy.

Investments

The next major area of money management requiring the manager's attention is investments. Almost everyone has some preconceived idea of what they'd like to do if they suddenly were wealthy. It might be oil investments, land, or stocks or bonds. Regardless of the area of interest, they're all investments. The successful artist must realize that entertainment, by its very nature, is a feast or famine business that won't last forever. With this thought in mind, the artist would be wise to construct an investment portfolio to counteract the uncertainty of his career in entertainment. Of course, this is relative, depending on just how successful the artist has been and the amount of wealth he's accumulated.

Needless to say, the artist would be well advised to consider the assistance of an investment counselor. There are investment firms specializing in stock and bonds, real estate, or almost any other area of interest. The large lending institutions and insurance companies offer investment counseling to their customers. Whatever the choice, the artist should know what he wants from the investment: Guaranteed earnings? Diversification? Is he a risk averter or taker? What does the artist want his investments to do for him?

Tax Planning

Closely linked to investments is tax planning. For artists in the high income brackets, their investments are greatly influenced by their tax exposure. Investments sheltering income from taxes may be more attractive to some artists, even though the rate of return or potential profit margin is less than others.

Probably the greatest enemy of the successful artist is the Internal Revenue Service. However, this formidable adversary can be minimized by professional tax planning and money management. The advice of a certified public accountant or professional tax planner is absolutely necessary. Because most artists' income is concentrated in a limited time period, their potential for tax exposure is great. It's therefore imperative that as much of the earnings as possible be shielded from income-tax liability. Tax avoidance is not tax evasion. In order to know exactly where the artist stands with the Internal Revenue Service, the services of an accountant should be used during all phases of the artist's career. One of the most unfortunate situations that can occur is for an artist to finally achieve success, only to receive a visit from the IRS for back taxes due to filing improper income tax returns, or in some instances, failure to file any return. The artist and manager who bury their heads in the sand hoping that the IRS will go away are taking a foolhardy approach. No matter what the amount of income the artist makes, he should file the proper tax returns. All supporting documents necessary to substantiate the tax return should be preserved. The importance of accurate record-keeping is magnified in light of a tax audit. The artist who maintains a good accounting system watched over by professionals is less likely to encounter problems with the taxing authorities than the artist who disregards record-keeping and accounting altogether.

Planning for Retirement

Also linked with investments, but extremely specialized in nature and serving a specific purpose, is a retirement plan for the artist. The investment portfolio can be constructed in such a way that certain investments will mature at a desired time, namely at retirement. On the other hand, investing with the primary purpose of retirement in mind would tend to limit investment opportunities. The artist should think of retirement as a specific part of his overall financial plan. Again, the advice of the accountant or investment counselor can be helpful in determining what can be expected from social security, union pension funds, or investments made specifically for retirement purposes. In addition, the artist's standard of living, dependents, and overall economic retirement needs should be analyzed. Based on these findings, a determination can be made regarding which course of action is necessary to provide the artist with an adequate retirement fund.

Estate Planning

Estate planning is the last major area of money management to be discussed. This area is concerned with the distribution of the artist's assets (after payment of all liabilities) to designated heirs. Unless an estate plan is implemented, the laws of the state in which the artist dies or where his property is located will dictate who will inherit his assets. The will is the legal instrument used to convey instructions regarding the distribution of the deceased party's assets. Failure to leave a will can sometimes work terrible hardship on loved ones.

There are serious economic consequences that can befall a person's estate if a will isn't left or if it's written improperly. By the use of the marital deduction, trusts, and other legal devices, sizeable amounts of money can be diverted from federal and state taxing authorities to family and friends. In addition to economic provisions, a properly drawn will can make provisions for guardianship of minor children, specific bequests, and other extraordinary transactions, such as gifts to charitable institutions.

The attorney drafting the artist's will should consult with the accountant and investment advisor in order to accumulate a complete set of facts about his client's economic picture and any special bequests. The will should be reviewed annually to determine if any modifications should be made due to changed circumstances. If the artist is married, it's advisable that the spouse also execute a will.

Certain investments also can influence the estate plan. For instance, life insurance is frequently used to add liquidity to an estate. Joint ownership of properties, charitable donations, and gifts are a few of the other avenues available to the financial planner in structuring the estate.

Summary

The artist and manager should approach the financial or money management part of the overall plan with caution. This includes an awareness of the necessity of debt, its proper use and control, and keeping a watchful eye on the amount of debt and spending habits of the artist. The manager must maintain control over income and expense through the "roadsheets," budgets, profit-and-loss statement, and balance sheet.

It's also the manager's job to help the artist accumulate wealth. This is done by using the control devices just mentioned. Once money is earned, the next concern of the artist and manager is to preserve it. Here the emphasis is on tax planning and sheltering. Through investments, the artist's wealth should grow. The result should be sufficient funds to maintain a chosen lifestyle as well as an adequate retirement fund and a sizeable estate to help provide for loved ones. Accomplishing all of this is successful money management.

25.
Superstardom: What's Next?

The ultimate objective of every artist is to reach the rank of superstar. Needless to say, the artist's manager shares this goal. Achieving the status of superstar is the apex of artistic achievement. Many aspire to become superstars, but few ever make it. There are a multitude of traps and barriers on the way up the career ladder. Even an artist's own success can keep him from ever becoming one of the greats in the world of entertainment. Superstardom is reserved only for the fortunate few who possess the rare combination of unique talent, artistic and business vision, single-minded drive, and blind luck.

The journey toward superstardom usually begins with that sudden desire to develop one's singing ability or learn to play a musical instrument. This first encounter often leads to thoughts of entertaining professionally. Many attempting a career in the entertainment business don't continue either due to a lack of talent or the desire and discipline necessary to master their ambition. For the individuals who do choose show business as a profession, the dropout rate is high. The stress of irregular hours, constant traveling, seemingly endless rejection and disappointment, and the realization that the entertainment business is not a get-rich-quick proposition, force many artists to pursue other careers. Those artists remaining find themselves fiercely competing for the available slots on the rosters of record companies, booking agencies, publishing, and management firms. Unfortunately, only a few artists achieve even this level of success because of the substantial investment required to develop and promote a new artist.

Even after an artist convinces a record company, agent, publisher, and manager that his talents have the potential for being profitably marketed, success is still not guaranteed. The artist and his development team must still face the judgment of the public if he's to continue his climb toward superstardom.

Even a measure of public acclaim is not sufficient. To everyone but the hardcore fan, the artist is only as good as what he does today. Yesterdays don't count. There's constant pressure to keep recording hit records or to continue writing quality songs. Many can't stand up to the test and eventually fade back into obscurity.

Even for those who can meet the creative challenge, there are other barriers. Age is an everpresent adversary to the aspiring superstar. In many instances, the entertainment industry places a premium on youth: "You'd better make it today, tomorrow might be too late." The changing tastes of the public is yet another trap that has ended any chance of superstardom for many. Then, as we've seen in an earlier chapter, success itself can be an artist's undoing. Too much glamour, fame, and money in too short a time can destroy the artist unable to cope with these elements of a success crisis.

For those few fortunate artists who have achieved the artistic and financial fulfillment that accompanies superstardom, can there be any challenges remaining? Believe it or not, this can be a troubling question to one who's "done it all."

In order to "make it," in addition to talent, appeal, and style, the superstar artist must have a special drive that allows him to keep going when others would give up. He must be a dreamer who seeks the unobtainable goal and is not afraid of attempting the impossible. Once the superstar artist succeds in turning his wildest dreams into realities, there's a void. He has never been programmed to slow down or lay back. At this point, he needs new goals, new projects, and new directions for his life. The superstar artist's manager can play an important role in helping the artist begin this new stage in his life.

While this type of situation can potentially present problems, it doesn't have to. The superstar artist should appreciate one very important aspect of his life shared by only a few in this world: he has achieved total financial security. This, along with his fame, maturity, and personal contacts, allow him to take his life, both personally and professionally, in whatever direction he chooses. The best advice any manager could give to a client in this situation is simply, "Enjoy whatever you decide to do."

The alternatives available to the superstar are limitless. Many choose to keep performing, recording, and writing. Their status gives them the freedom to expand artistically. They can choose the dates they want to play without giving primary emphasis to the money involved. They have more freedom of choice in the records they'll release and the songs they'll write. They can pace their careers to get more enjoyment out of the things they do rather than be controlled by the pressures of having to "make it."

Superstardom affords the artist the financial capability and business contacts to get involved as an entertainment entrepreneur. Many highly successful artists have involved themselves in launching new record labels, motion picture productions, recording studios, publishing firms, booking agencies, or management companies.

Many others have used their fame and fortune in non-show business-related ventures, including real estate and other business investments.

Besides continued career fulfillment and business activities, an artist's stature and financial stability allow him to get involved in charitable causes by giving benefit concerts or acting as a spokesman for a particular charitable organization.

Many superstars use their financial security to develop themselves through other endeavors such as writing, lecturing, and travel. This also allows them the time to develop closer bonds with their families without the pressures of having to leave home for a tour or a recording date.

Summary

We've seen how superstardom affects an artist and his career. We've also seen how the artist's success affects another very important person, his manager. The superstar success of the artist-client also translates into superstar status for the manager in business circles of the industry. Beyond the financial rewards and respect for the manager by others in the entertainment industry, the superstar's manager can count on his client being a sure-fire drawing card for other promising artists seeking quality management. The old adage that "nothing succeeds like success" is certainly applicable to the career of the superstar manager.

The label "superstar" fits only a few, yet it's the goal of every artist who has ever called himself a professional entertainer. No matter what level of artistic achievement or financial success an artist attains over the span of his career, the ultimate goals are the same, just as are the motivational factors.

Throughout the book we've stressed that entertainment is a business just as sophisticated and complex as any other potentially lucrative endeavor. The artist striving to be tomorrow's superstar should never forget this.

Besides the financial reward and satisfaction that goes with achievement and a job well done, the entertainment business offers everyone connected with it that certain extra indefinable quality that makes people do whatever is necessary just to stay close to it. Call it "Sawdust in Your Shoes" or the "Smell of Greasepaint and the Roar of the Crowd," but whatever it is, it gets in your blood, it quickens your pulse, and it makes all the headaches somehow seem worthwhile. As any artist, manager, or other industry professional will undoubtedly tell you, "There's no business like show business."

Index

Edited by Bonnie Silverstein
Designed by Jay Anning
Set in 12-point Helvetica Light

DATE DUE

Feb 1 4:11 pm		
Feb 2 4:26		
15 7:34		
Feb 21 6		
Mar. 13 6:54 pm		
Apr. 2 9:00 an		
Apr. 2 10:16 pm		
JUL 2 4 1996		

Brodart Co.   Cat. # 55 137 001   Printed in USA